THE CROSS-CULTURAL PARTNERSHIP SURVIVAL GUIDE

Proven Steps for Launching Healthy
Partnerships between Churches of
Different Cultures

JOHN WESLEY YODER

The Cross-Cultural Partnership Survival Guide

Copyright © 2024 by John Wesley Yoder

Scripture quotations are taken from The Holy Bible, English Standard Version® ESV®

Publisher Information

John Wesley Yoder

Plymouth, Minnesota

For more information or to contact the author, please email john@immigrantministry.com.

ISBN 979-8-9901378-0-6 (softcover)

ISBN 979-8-9901378-1-3 (hardcover)

ISBN 979-8-9901378-2-0 (ebook)

Cover design: Terry Dugan

Cover illustration: Casoalfonso @ Adobe Stock

Interior design: Ben Wolf, Inc.

Editing: Josh Vogt

Publishing services provided by BelieversBookServices.com

First printing: 2024

Printed in the United States of America

Story-driven and engaging to read, Yoder's quick start guide to cross-cultural partnerships between churches is biblically-grounded, practically-focused wisdom shared by a seasoned practitioner. If you desire to see your church pursue partnership in this way but don't have time to wade through the complex theory and missiological jargon of textbooks prepared for cross-cultural missionaries, this resource was designed for you!

Jessica A. Udall, PhD
Professor of Intercultural Studies at Evangelical Theological College (Addis Ababa, Ethiopia), adjunct professor of Intercultural Studies at Columbia International University (Columbia, SC, USA), author of *Loving the Stranger: Welcoming Immigrants in the Name of Jesus*

As a Malawian living in Britain, I see remarkable similarities in relationships between native-born and immigrant pastors on both sides of the Atlantic. You will find in this book an insightful story that explores key aspects of multicultural ministry in the age of migration. John Wesley Yoder has used the gift of storytelling to help understand the opportunities and challenges that come with the presence of brothers and sisters of other ethnicities and from other parts of the world in our cities and communities. The story itself is powerful. The experiences of those involved are eye-opening. I could not help but root for Susan…she nails it in the end. The wisdom shared is profound. Everyone involved in multicultural ministry will find this book helpful.

Dr. Harvey Kwyiani
Chief Executive Officer, Global Connections

If God has put in your heart the need to connect with our family in Christ from other nations that are found here in

North America and work together as the Body of Christ that we are; This is the book for you. With an easy-to-follow fictional narrative, stories from John's personal journey and practical application steps that I found to be my favorite part of the book, you'll be hard pressed to find another like it.

Carlos O. Negron
Director of Church Engagement, MissioNexus

This is the book I needed when I first launched into cross-cultural ministry. Its accessible language makes it a joy to read, and its Application Study Guide will walk any church leadership team through the steps necessary to build a healthy cross-cultural partnership. I cannot recommend this book highly enough.

Russell Mann
Cross-Cultural Student Minister
Central Baptist Church, Decatur, Alabama

As someone deeply rooted in pastoral ministry and familiar with the challenges and blessings of cross-cultural engagement, I found 'The Cross-Cultural Partnership Survival Guide' a profoundly insightful and necessary resource. John skillfully navigates the complexities of fostering healthy relationships between American and immigrant churches, offering practical guidance and real-world examples. This book resonates with my own experiences and echoes the essential call for mutual understanding and collaboration in our increasingly multicultural Christian landscape. It is a must-read anyone seeking to build bridges and serve effectively in diverse ministry contexts. I'm excited to see how God will use the immigrant church in the Kingdom's work in the United States.

Sam Chacko
Lead Pastor, LOFT City Church, Richardson, Texas
New Church Start Up Coach, | Stadia Church Planting

Multicultural church partnerships are difficult, but based on many years of experience and research, John Wesley Yoder explains the practices of those who have done it well. As he tells his own story, he articulates a healthy set of principles that increase the likelihood of building a healthy partnership.

After years of interviewing leaders from many cultures, John wrote this book to benefit not only native-born American pastors, but also congregations of immigrants trying to partner with them. I have read many books on this topic, looking for help as a Hispanic pastor serving in a multicultural context, but this book rises to the top of the list because it is based primarily on personal experience rather than bibliographic research.

Dr. Enrique Fernandez
Director of Contextual Studies Department
Latin America Training Network

You have to understand the ABC's before you can speak the language and communicate the message. John Wesley Yoder brings a practical application of the basics of intercultural ministry in the local church. The power of this book is that it brings practical education and applicable steps to succeed in ministry for your local congregation. Based on years of experience, Yoder's easy to read style will take away the fear you might have in engaging the diversity around you and your church. This is a call to enter into a amazing adventure by embracing ethnic congregations into your local scene.

Rick Ryan
Executive Director of Intercultural Ministries
Arizona Ministry Network of the Assemblies of God

This book is simple, practical, powerful, and timely. Cross-cultural partnership is the key to the current era of mission. Yet we find the church often unable to establish the sort of relationships that lead to real traction. John builds on years of experience in the trenches to help you get started in the strategic opportunity of our day.

Ted Esler, PhD
President Missio Nexus

This book is for everyone who has a love for those who make up the *great multitude which no one can count from every tribe, nation, people and language*, whom St. John's Revelation pictures before the Throne and the Lamb. I wish I had this book and the wisdom found here years ago as I began to discover the joys and challenges of working with immigrant leaders. John's protagonist, Susan, asks the question which so many of us have asked, "What would it take for everyday American Christians to **want** to learn to build friendships with Christians from around the world? And then to actually build those relationships?" Here you will find the answer to these questions in completely understandable and practical language. If you are asking those questions, this book will be immensely helpful! The study guide which is included will be most useful for individuals and teams as churches work to demonstrate the Revelation 7:9 reality in their context.

Rev. Dr. Peter A. Meier
Executive Director, Missions and Outreach
Florida-Georgia District LCMS

Thirty years ago when we embarked upon the journey of growing a multicultural church and eventually a multi congregational family of churches it would have been very helpful to have a resource like this book. John Yoder uses a compelling story combined with practical principles and practices to help equip and empower those who are just beginning this journey or those who are already on their way. I highly recommend it.

Rev. Dr. Jim Olson
Former Senior Pastor of Bethel Christian Fellowship
and Founder of the All Nations Family of Churches

As the sole pastor of a "North American" church in South Florida, the opportunities to partner with immigrant churches are numerous. Finally, there is a practical resource that will help everyday pastors and lay leaders understand what it takes to form a healthy partnership with a church from another culture! This book and the included strategy guides have become a great resource for me and our partner congregations.

Rev. Jacob Roedsens
Pastor, Our Savior Lutheran Church
Lake Worth Beach, Florida

As a 1.5-generation Hmong immigrant to the United States who coaches immigrant congregations within Anglo-American churches, I've considered writing my thoughts for the benefit of others. John Wesley Yoder beat me in writing everything I wanted to say in *The Cross-Cultural Partnership Survival Guide*. Thank you, John, for doing the hard work for me!

Vue Lee

Assistant to the President for Missions
Lutheran Church Missouri Synod, Minnesota South District

Finally! A practical guide for church leaders wishing for specific steps and guidance to enable their ministry to their local international neighbors! Yoder gives much-needed simple guidance that the local church urgently seeks while missiologists continue the vital study of diaspora and globalization issues. While resources abound assisting churches dealing with a racial divide, fewer resources currently exist to assist in dealing with a language divide. In this work, Yoder points us to the vital key to local church cross-cultural ministry fruit: A healthy partnership between a local American majority church and a local immigrant church.

Matthew Gregory
People Groups Strategist
Southern Baptist Convention of Virginia

As a missions pastor, I have had the privilege of watching John Wesley Yoder develop into an expert and leading voice in the area of cross-cultural church partnerships. I highly recommend *The Cross-Cultural Partnership Survival Guide* to anyone desiring concrete action steps to improve their church's intercultural partnership capacity.

Chaz Nichols
Asia Director, Converge International Ministries

Puzzled how your primarily monocultural church can possibly comply with Christ's high priestly prayer that all believers – including believers from differing cultures – should reflect the unity of His body?

John Yoder has good news for you! Having attended services of at least 80 primarily immigrant churches in the US, and had coffee or lunch with most of their pastors, the Lord has given John deep insights into how partnerships between churches of differing cultures can powerfully demonstrate the love of Christ and the unity of His body.

Written in an engaging, relatable manner, this book will inspire and equip you and your church - step by small, manageable step - toward winsome biblical unity with local believers of another culture. Observing this newfound unity across cultural siloes, believers in your community may be drawn to Christ - who alone enables us to venture out of our monocultural comfort zones toward that unity that elevates Him!

Pat Hatch
Refugee and Immigrant Ministry Director
Presbyterian Church in America (PCA) Mission to North America

This book addresses some key challenges associated with cross-cultural church partnerships with insight from the author's personal experiences. The three "Quick Start Guidelines" provide practical solutions to these challenges, highlighting how to address differences between cultures, between generations, and between denominations.

Harold Roesler
World Impact missionary (retired)

Contents

Cross-Cultural Ministry Bewilders an Outreach Director

S usan Jamison fought against the nauseating mix of confusion and betrayal in her stomach. Earlier that week, she had such a wonderful meeting with Pastor Mateo Ruiz. A gracious Ecuadorian, Pastor Ruiz had a clearly orthodox statement of faith and a personal recommendation from Pastor Alfonso Hernandez, whom Susan deeply respected.

Although she was only two months into her new role forming cross-cultural partnerships for her church and district, Susan had enough positive experiences under her belt to feel confident inviting three of her church's elders to attend Pastor Ruiz's new congregation. The length and loudness of the sermon didn't bother her. That was just cultural, and she felt confident the elders could look past it. But what about the message Pastor Ruiz spoke to his congregation?

Pastor Ruiz scolded his people. "If you do not pay your tithes for me to be your full-time pastor, who will pray for your children when they are sick? Who will cast the demons out of your new homes?"

Uh-oh, Susan thought. *This will not sit well with the elders.*

Susan glanced down at the bulletin. The front page announced, "If anyone brings ten new members into the church, they will receive a *free* used car!" Susan cringed to think what would happen if anybody printed that in the Fragrant Hills Church bulletin.

Pastor Ruiz continued, "Today's offering is not adequate. God's people must step out in faith if they want to see His blessing in their lives! We are going to take the offering again, and we will keep taking it until the needs of the church are met!"

On cue, the pianist launched into another rendition of her offering song. As before, members of the congregation came forward one-by-one, placing their offerings in the slot of the ornate gold-colored chest at the front of the platform. As each donation was dropped into the box, the congregation clapped and shouted a hearty "Amen!" To Susan's relief, the announcement was soon made that the second offering had met the church's needs.

The elders sat politely through the rest of the service and greeted people afterwards. Only after they reached the parking lot could Susan open up with them.

"I am so sorry! I had no idea Pastor Ruiz's preaching was like this. He came so well recommended by Pastor Hernandez, and he was nothing like this when we had lunch together."

One of the elders tried to reassure her. "Susan, we don't hold you responsible for any of this. That wasn't you on the platform. We know this is all new to you, and you'll figure it out over time." The others were just as gracious.

But Susan knew she had royally blown it. This seemed like a major setback for cross-cultural ministry at Fragrant Hills. What if she lacked any real competence for this new position? Why had she taken it in the first place?

It all began two months before, when Pastor Jeremy Metcalf invited Susan and her husband Bill to a Saturday workshop at the Great Lakes district office of the Parkerite Church. The speaker was Sonia Patel, who had been hired the year before as the first Multicultural Partnership Catalyst for the Parkerite Church. This was Sonia's first visit to the Great Lakes district. Earlier that week, she had been meeting with district pastors and other staff. On Saturday, the district organized an afternoon event and invited laypeople from Columbus area churches.

District Superintendent Grant McNamara introduced Sonia. "For twelve years running, we Parkerites have won the award for being America's whitest denomination!" Several in the crowd laughed. Susan wasn't sure how many members of Fragrant Hills would find his joke particularly amusing. "I don't know if anyone keeps such statistics, but we might also be America's most rapidly declining denomination. Our current projections show that within forty years, the only place you will be able to find a Parkerite church is on the other side of the pearly gates.

For some time, our national leadership has been concerned about the decline of American Christianity and the Parkerite Church in particular. But we've largely ignored the waves of immigration that have reshaped our communities over the past thirty years. A visit to Walmart in any city of our district will quickly demonstrate that the makeup of our communities has changed. But the makeup of our churches hasn't.

Many Christians see this as an opportunity to share the gospel with Muslims and others who have little opportunity to hear the gospel in their homelands. I share their vision. But there is another aspect of immigration we've overlooked. God has brought millions of devout Christians from around the world to the U.S. Thousands of them are pastors, and they've launched churches all around us. Yet even though we are neighbors, we don't know one another, and don't serve the Kingdom together. That needs to change.

One of headquarters' best moves in the past year is to hire Sonia Patel as our first-ever Multicultural Ministry Catalyst. Sonia comes to us with impeccable credentials. She is Director of Human Resources for DataConnect, an international Indian-based tech firm with offices in seventeen countries. Her family has lived near the San Diego office for eight years now. Her husband is one of the elders at Miramar Hindi Fellowship, one of the first Indian congregations to join the Parkerites. We are so grateful she has committed eight hours per week to serve as our Multicultural Ministry Catalyst.

For the past three days, she's been interacting with our Great Lakes District pastors about the cross-cultural church partnerships that have been forming in the San Diego area. We've learned a lot from her experiences and want to see our churches launch into similar partnerships in the upcoming months. It's my privilege to introduce her to you now."

"Greetings everyone!" Sonia said. "I've really enjoyed the time I've spent with Great Lakes leadership these past days. Some have joked because I'm the only Indian here, I'm like the caramel syrup on top of your vanilla sundae. Fair enough. Well, you're all invited to worship with us at

Miramar Hindi Fellowship, where you can be the cream in our coffee.

It is always refreshing for me to spend time with wonderful Christian leaders like you. I spend most of my time traveling globally to train HR managers in building strong dynamics among culturally diverse teams. At DataConnect, the motivation that brings all of us together is financial profit. But we Parkerites are quite different—our bottom line isn't money but the expansion of the Kingdom of God."

Sonia spoke with graciousness and camaraderie as she addressed the ministry leaders of the Great Lakes district. But it was clear from her business suit and perfectly coiffed hair that she functioned daily in the executive class. Susan felt gratitude that the Parkerites had found someone so experienced who was willing to lead its cross-cultural initiative.

"Grant was very gracious in introducing me. But I want to set your expectations appropriately. I know how to train corporate businesspeople to work effectively in cross-cultural teams. But I don't have experience in the nonprofit sector. I haven't yet figured out what motivates pastors and everyday Christians to desire cross-cultural relationships when their only motivation is their love for Christ and each other. I wish I could guarantee I will turn the Parkerite ship around. We'll have to wait and see.

I know that most white Parkerite churches are monocultural. So is Miramar Hindi Fellowship and most of the other immigrant churches I've experienced. The members of our church are good, Christ-honoring people, and they're not racists. But they have to function in an American world all week, and Sunday is like a special treat when they get to speak Hindi, sing familiar songs, and stay for tikka masala afterwards. We can't imagine why we would want to change that to fellowship with a bunch of whites or Latinos or anyone else. And as I worship with whites and Latinos, their feelings are the same. Money is the incentive that drives different nationalities to collaborate at DataConnect. It's hard for me to identify a common motivator that works with churches of different nationalities.

One day I was driving thirteen-year-old Anushka home from soccer practice when she said, 'Mom, if I have to go to church on Sunday, can I go to River Crest Parkerite instead of Miramar Hindi?' She had attended several youth events at River Crest and built friendships there. We had hoped she would learn Hindi well enough to understand our pastor's sermons, but that hasn't happened. So she sits bored in church, surfing the Web on her phone. That led her father and I to have a difficult conversation, 'Is it more important for our daughter to go to Miramar Hindi Fellowship, or to heaven?'

I've discovered that Nigerians, Koreans, Russians, and others face the same problem. Like us, they prefer to avoid asking the question. Grant has shared with you honestly why the Parkerite white majority is slow to adopt multicultural ministry. Well, the rest of us are just as slow.

I wish I could tell you I have all the answers. Right now, I feel like I'm trying to identify the right questions. At a minimum, I can tell you we're all in trouble if we don't learn to work together. Let me share some details."

For the next 20 minutes, Sonia walked the audience through a well-organized series of graphs and charts. Four charts vividly portrayed the decline of American Christianity, mainline denominations, the Parkerite Church and even the Great Lakes district. The next series of pie charts portrayed levels of immigration to America, Christian immigrants in America, and the effectiveness of immigrant churches in disciple-making as compared to their American counterparts. She closed by sharing the story of Kindred Spirit Church, a thriving second-plus-generation Latino congregation in San Diego.

"So you see," said Sonia, "there are a few marvelous stories of ministry partnerships even among us Parkerites. The ones I've seen so far are in Southern California. My role is to see such partnerships flourish in every district like yours. Thanks for listening, and I hope our relationship will be long and productive." Sonia closed her presentation with several minutes of questions and answers from the audience.

After the session ended, Pastor Jeremy said to Bill and Susan, "Why don't you grab some coffee and muffins in the lobby, and then head to Meeting Room A? I'd like you to have a few minutes with Sonia and Grant." A few minutes later, Bill and Susan seated themselves at the long rectangular table in Meeting Room A. They thought a group of people might be gathering to engage further with Sonia. But the only people who joined them were Pastor Jeremy, Sonia and Grant.

Pastor Jeremy began, "You know, Bill and Susan, we've wanted to begin reaching out into the ethnic communities that have sprung up across Columbus. But that's a big stretch for our people, and they wouldn't know where to start. These last few days, I've had very constructive conversations with Grant about launching into multicultural ministry at Fragrant Hills. Grant, would you like to share what we've discussed?"

Bill and Susan didn't know Grant personally, but had heard him speak as their district superintendent. They were glad he was exposing Pastor Jeremy to resources beyond Fragrant Hills.

"We've wanted to focus on cross-cultural ministry here in the district for some time," Grant began. "But we've always been short-staffed. Our staff have multiple responsibilities, and many are providing pastoral ministry in addition to district leadership. We simply haven't had anyone with bandwidth to focus on cross-cultural partnerships.

This week Sonia has offered our district a three-year grant from headquarters. The grant allows us to hire someone eight hours per week as a Multicultural Partnership Catalyst, a role similar to hers. Half of that time will be focused on ministries across the district. But the other half will be focused on developing one local church as a prototype of healthy cross-cultural partnerships. Sonia will personally coach the person who takes this new role. We want to see role models across the country as well as in San Diego. So I approached Pastor Jeremy about the possibility of Fragrant Hills becoming our pilot project, and our hiring a Catalyst from within Fragrant Hills."

"Susan, you're the first person I thought of," said Pastor Jeremy. "I'd like you to seriously consider taking the role and initiating cross-cultural partnerships at Fragrant Hills as well as across the district."

Susan's jaw dropped. "Me?" she asked. "I'm just an accountant! I don't have any experience with cross-cultural ministry."

Susan and Bill were as monoculturally American as you can get. They had attended Fragrant Hills since their courtship at Ohio State. Bill majored in information systems and Susan in accounting. Their wedding portrait could have served as the inspiration for a Norman Rockwell painting. All three of their children came to faith and were baptized at Fragrant Hills. They couldn't imagine worshipping anywhere else.

But everyone knew Fragrant Hills was graying. There was concern that within ten years, the church might not have enough young people to sustain children's or youth ministries. Bill and Susan were heartbroken that two of their three adult children had no interest whatsoever in church. Nate, their youngest, maintained his childhood passion for Christ, but had left for a more contemporary church on the other side of Columbus. Everyone at Fragrant Hills was asking what they might do to revitalize the church.

Bill and Susan clearly resonated with Sonia's vision. But Susan repeated her objection. "I'm just an accountant with no cross-cultural experience to qualify me for this job."

Pastor Jeremy reminded Susan about her ministry through InterVarsity during her years at Ohio State. Susan remembered her experiences fondly. She had befriended mostly Korean and Chinese students. She really enjoyed helping them obtain cell phone service, figure out bus schedules, and especially how to eat waffles with a knife and fork. She had led two Korean girls to faith in Christ—one of the highlights of her college experience. Though both girls had moved to other states, they stayed in contact with Susan over social media. Susan knew they were still actively involved in local churches.

Those were wonderful memories. But Susan felt they hardly qualified her to build relationships with pastors from around the world. Sonia spoke a few words to assure her. "Susan, I work in HR. I don't 'get' ministry. I don't know how pastors think, and what would motivate them to desire partnerships. I'm learning by doing and making lots of mistakes. What I know about building cross-cultural relationship building is that it comes down to asking good questions and patiently listening.

We realize this is completely new to you. None of us want to pressure you for a decision. I'm in town for another day, and tomorrow afternoon I'll be worshipping with the first Latino congregation in the Great Lakes district, La Luz del Mundo. They will provide English translation. Would the two of you be willing to join me for that service?"

Susan and Bill looked at each other, and quickly nodded consent. They enjoyed meeting with international students during their college days, and thought Latino worship might be really enjoyable.

The following afternoon, Susan and Bill found themselves driving into the parking lot of La Luz del Mundo. They had no idea what to expect, but were pleasantly surprised. The congregation numbered about 45, mostly young couples with lots of babies and young children. Everyone was very friendly, though many spoke limited English. The service was almost two hours in length. The music was lively, vivacious, and fun. Susan noticed the absence of any songbooks or projected lyrics. Everyone knew the words and sang them with spirit. A woman named Maria sat between Susan and Bill and translated for them during Pastor Alfonso's sermon.

His message was simple and biblical. "A woman had an illness that caused a flow of blood. She walked up behind Jesus and touched his clothes. Although he was surrounded by a big crowd, Jesus felt her faith. He turned to her and said, 'Your faith makes you well.'" Then Pastor Alfonso brought his message home: "Jesus can heal you, too. Some of you are sick. Some of you need to be healed from alcohol or drugs. Some of you need healing for your marriage. You need to have faith like that woman. Cry out to Jesus for help! He will see your faith. He will turn to you. He will make you well too. That's how Jesus is. He sees us and loves us. He receives anybody who comes to him. Don't wait! Have faith in him!"

At the end of his message, Pastors Alfonso and Victoria invited anyone who wanted prayer to come to the front of the auditorium. To Susan's surprise, most of the congregation got up and walked to the front. She and Bill watched as one by one, Pastors Alfonso and Victoria laid their hands on the shoulder of each person and prayed over them.

Unexpectedly, Pastor Victoria walked up to Susan and placed her hands on Susan's shoulder, praying for her. Susan was greatly touched. She hadn't gone forward for prayer. She didn't know anyone in the congregation. And she clearly wasn't Latino. That didn't faze Pastor Victoria. Susan wasn't sure what her prayer was all about, but had confidence the Holy Spirit spoke good Spanish. Susan felt loved.

She realized that Pastor Alfonso might not be the world's greatest Bible teacher, but he and his wife deeply loved and cared for their flock. Their devout faith and spiritual giftedness were unmistakable.

Susan was hooked. She *had* to do this. She *had* to be part of God's work among the nations in Columbus. Plus, the thought of being personally mentored by Sonia was exciting —if a bit intimidating.

The next morning, Susan emailed Sonia, Grant and Jeremy to say she would accept the position. She knew it lacked definition. Sonia recommended that she spend her initial weeks getting to know the three immigrant congregations that were considering relationships with the district.

Susan already knew she loved the people of La Luz del Mundo. Drawing closer to them would be a delight. She was thrilled by the teachable spirit she sensed in Pastors Alfonso and Victoria. Although neither had finished high school, they were both eager to begin the online video-based Spanish theological training for which the district had provided a scholarship. Susan clearly observed that the quality of their preaching improved month after month. So did their English. They knew that English would be the heart language of their children. They wanted to lead a Latino church that would be relevant to future generations.

Susan also met Thang Nguyen, a Vietnamese mechanical engineer who was Vice President of Iron Hull Naval Systems, a defense contractor with the U.S. Navy. He was also pastor of Hoi Thanh Church, part of the Christian and Missionary Alliance. With 40 in regular attendance, Hoi Thanh had outgrown its current meeting space, and had begun to dialogue with Pastor Jeremy about the use of the Fragrant Hills facility on Sunday afternoons.

Susan had met African pastors in the area who were also well-educated and held professional jobs in healthcare, finance and marketing. However, the only African church expressing interest in partnership with the Parkerites was the Columbus South Sudanese Church. It took some time for Susan to connect with Pastor Rashed Gerang. Like the rest of his congregation, Pastor Gerang was a refugee who had recently arrived from South Sudan. Lacking formal education, most of the congregation worked one or two jobs just to pay their bills. They made time on Sunday afternoons to meet at Pastor Gerang's home for worship. It was unclear whether they would pursue a facility for worship. Because of his busy work schedule, Susan needed to wait for Pastor Gerang to tell her when he would be available to meet.

As Susan met more people from different cultures, she grasped the complexity of modern American culture. She felt increasingly overwhelmed by the task. Yet she felt deep affection for the global brothers and sisters she was meeting. Their prayer gatherings resounded with passion and zeal exceeding that of most American congregations.

When Pastor Alfonso told her that his friend Pastor Ruiz was launching another congregation across town, Susan naively assumed this new congregation would be as healthy as the ones she'd previously encountered. She knew that sharing a meal was the best way to start a new relationship, so she asked for Pastor Ruiz's contact information. Before long, she had scheduled a lunch meeting with him and his wife.

Despite the promising start, now she'd been mortified by the manipulative, authoritarian preaching that had unfolded. Despite her due diligence with Pastor Ruiz and however gracious the Fragrant Hills elders might be, this presented a hard setback for promoting cross-cultural partnerships among the congregation.

Needing to debrief, Susan scheduled a call with Sonia, already formulating the words of a gracious resignation.

The next Sunday at Fragrant Hills, Susan looked around the room. Although it was the same congregation she'd always known, she realized now how monocultural they were. While Susan realized she had a lot of growing to do, she also knew she had more cross-cultural savvy than anyone else in the church. If she struggled to build relationships with immigrant Christians, what hope did they have?

Susan regretted that not only did most of her Christian friends lack the skills to befriend people from other cultures, they also lacked any real desire to do so. Although she wanted to resign from her position, a burden had seized her heart to see healthy ministry partnerships raised up among the many ethnicities in Columbus. This passion proved stronger than her fears.

That evening, Susan couldn't sleep. So many thoughts swam around in her head. She and Bill were grieving over their two adult children that had no interest in spiritual things. Pastors of these immigrant churches certainly had the same concerns for their own children. What could she do about spiritual toxicity of Pastor Ruiz's church? What about the great cultural diversity she had experienced? What would it take for everyday American Christians to **want** to learn to build friendships with Christians from around the world? And then to follow through?

Susan got up to read her Bible, seeking a passage offering comfort and reassurance. Instead, she discovered the story of New Testament believers who were every bit as perplexed about cross-cultural ministry as her.

2

Cross-Cultural Ministry
Bewildered the Early Church

U nable to sleep, Susan got up to read her Bible. The previous week, she had begun to read the Book of Acts. It was one of her favorite books in the Bible, because it talked about the start of the early church. Just the day before, she had read the story of Peter preaching to Cornelius the Centurion in Acts chapter 10. This amazing story recounted how the first group of Gentiles came to faith through Peter's preaching.

Susan began to read Acts chapter 11, which continued the story as Peter told a group of Jewish believers about his experience at Cornelius' home. In verse 18, Susan realized she was looking at a picture, not only of herself, but of many friends at Fragrant Hills: "When they heard these things, they fell silent. And they glorified God, saying, 'Then to the Gentiles also God has granted repentance that leads to life.'"

Peter's audience responded in two stages: first they fell silent, and *then* they glorified God. As an all-Jewish audience, they already understood that Jesus wanted to save Jews. It was a stretch for them to think Jesus also wanted to save Samaritans. But Cornelius? Cornelius was an Italian. An

Italian! Worse, he was a Roman centurion, part of the military machine that oppressed the Jewish people. And God wanted to save *them*?

This Jewish audience didn't immediately glorify God. At first, they fell silent. Susan imagined an hourglass icon spinning on her phone when she clicked a slow link. She could visualize that hourglass spinning in the eyes of those Jewish people as they repeated to themselves:

- God loves Italians?
- God loves Italians?
- God loves Italians?
- God loves Italians!

After repeating it to themselves quietly in their heads, they finally could praise God for the salvation of Cornelius' household.

These Jewish people struggled because this news fell completely outside of their paradigm. And the news Susan needed to deliver to the people of Fragrant Hills would be totally outside their paradigm as well.

Faithful Parkerites revered great heroes of American church history, but failed to realize these spiritual leaders were all white folks like them. The unspoken expectation was that God would continue to send great awakenings to the American church exclusively through white people.

However, churches whose members looked like their spiritual forbears were mostly in decline. Leaders of growing churches in modern America more likely had names like Gonzales, Wang, or Okeke. Parkerites would struggle to accept the new reality that God had brought millions of devout Christians from around the world to America, that thousands of them were pastors, and that they made disciples and planted churches faster than most white congregations.

In contrast, devout first-generation immigrant pastors would find it equally difficult to accept that they stood to lose the hearts of their children because they didn't disciple them in English or empower them for leadership as young adults. Susan knew it would take time for both groups to come to terms with these hard realities.

Then Susan thought back to the previous day's passage, Acts chapter 10. There, Peter saw the same vision twice. A blanket full of unclean animals descended from heaven, and the voice of God commanded, "Rise, kill, and eat." God didn't tell Peter at that time what the vision meant. Peter just knew that God had a major work in motion. That same afternoon, believers from Joppa came and asked him to preach at the household of a man by the name of Cornelius. And as he did, Cornelius and his entire household believed.

How did Peter and the Jews with him respond when they saw Cornelius and his household believe? Acts 10:45 tells us, "And the believers from among the circumcised who had come with Peter were amazed, because the gift of the Holy Spirit was poured out even on the Gentiles."

In other words, it shocked them. God wasn't working in the way they expected.

Peter preached a powerful message. He was an experienced evangelist who had delivered messages like this many times. But he didn't even get the chance to finish this time. As he spoke, verse 44 reveals: "While Peter was still saying these things, the Holy Spirit fell on all who heard the word." Verse 46 continues, "They were hearing them speaking in tongues and extolling God."

This is not the way American crusade preaching is supposed to work. In the middle of the message, without any altar call, the audience started speaking in tongues. No one asked them if they wanted to receive Jesus Christ as their personal Savior. No one prayed over them. No one laid hands on them. No one asked them if they wanted to speak in tongues. Nobody even asked them if they believed a word Peter said. As they heard, the Holy Spirit came upon them and they spoke in tongues. *How rude!* They didn't even let the evangelist finish his message.

Susan realized God was doing many unexpected things in America. God's expansion of the Kingdom through immigrant believers didn't fit how Americans envisioned, strategized, funded, or organized ministry. It was a work of God. Susan needed to bring this to the attention of the people of the Great Lakes district. They would need time to be surprised, to listen, and to process. Hopefully, most of them would come to praise God for His work among the nations that had come to the United States.

Susan thought back to Acts chapter 1, which told the story of the famous upper room prayer meeting of 120 followers of Jesus. Unlike the multiethnic revival that broke out in Acts chapter 2, the prayer meeting in Acts chapter 1 was remarkably monocultural. It warmed Susan's heart to be reminded that God shows up powerfully in united prayer by any group of His people, whether from one ethnicity or many. She longed for the day when Christians of many ethnicities joined the Parkerites in prayer, fellowship, and disciple-making, but she was at peace that God would hear the prayers of her denomination regardless of its ethnic composition.

Acts chapter 2 was one of her favorite chapters in the entire Bible—and Susan didn't have to be a Pentecostal to love that riveting passage. People from sixteen different ethnicities heard the gospel. The Holy Spirit fell on men and women, and upon young and old. Three thousand people came to faith and were baptized. A church was formed, and its people continued together daily in worship and fellowship. What's to not love?

As the next chapters covered a few months, the entire church remained in Jerusalem. The believers grew in number. They also grew in maturity and became a robust, healthy body. But the church was ingrown, because everyone stayed in Jerusalem until the end of Acts chapter 7, when Stephen was stoned. Susan read the words that followed in Acts 8:1: "Saul approved of his execution. And there arose on that day a great persecution against the church in Jerusalem, and they were all scattered throughout the regions of Judea and Samaria, except the apostles." Verse 4 continued, "Now those who were scattered went everywhere preaching the word."

Verse 1 said that they were *all* scattered, except the apostles. By that time the church had grown to well over 10,000 people, and there were only twelve apostles. That meant that *more than 99%* of the church of Jerusalem got kicked out of town.

In modern terms, their flight would be called *involuntary migration*. *Voluntary migration* refers to those who leave their homelands for work or study opportunities, or to be reunited with family members. *Involuntary migration* refers to those who flee war, drug lords, famine, drought, and other forms of violence and natural disasters. The Jerusalem Christians fled persecution. They were involuntary migrants. And the text said, "Those who were scattered went everywhere preaching the word."

Susan returned to Acts 11:19-21, realizing she'd missed something. "Now, those who were scattered because of the persecution that arose over Stephen traveled as far as Phoenicia and Cyprus and Antioch, speaking the word to no one except Jews. But there were some of them, men of Cyprus and Cyrene, who on coming to Antioch spoke to the Hellenists also preaching the Lord Jesus. And the hand of the Lord was with them, and a great number who believed turned to the Lord."

Susan remembered childhood sermons that highlighted spiritual leaders like Paul and Barnabas who were commissioned and sent forth by the church to proclaim the word. But these thousands of believers weren't officially commissioned and sent forth by anyone. They simply fled persecution.

Wow! I have got to share this with the people of Fragrant Hills! For some time, Susan had seen firsthand how God used marvelous believers from around the world to spread the gospel in Columbus. Now, this parallel history revealed that God had used migration in the New Testament to powerfully spread the gospel. Perhaps the scripture-loving Parkerites would find this an easier message to embrace.

This compelling perspective from the book of Acts helped Susan envision how she could speak convincingly to members of the Great Lakes district. It gave her enough peace of mind to settle down for a good night's sleep. She wanted to be well-rested for her Zoom call with Sonia Patel the following morning.

3

Cross-Cultural Ministry Bewilders an Entire Denomination

S usan was greatly relieved to have a Zoom conversation with Sonia. Susan realized how monocultural she was through her engagement with La Luz del Mundo. She knew she had made cultural blunders in developing her relationship with Pastors Alfonso and Victoria. She feared the level of cultural complexity would grow exponentially as she engaged with Vietnamese, South Sudanese and other global cultures. Adding to that complexity, she was beginning to discern the massive disconnect between the first and second generations of each culture.

Her stress level spiked with her frustration at bringing Fragrant Hills elders to attend Pastor Ruiz' service. Susan needed perspective, guidance, and hope. But before she would have capacity to receive any of these things, she needed to vent.

The steam off Susan's coffee matched the heat of her voice as she vented her growing frustrations. "This feels completely impossible! Every time I bring someone new into the conversation, it just complicates things more. People are so disconnected, even in their own churches."

Fortunately, Sonia proved a patient listener. She waited until Susan's torrent of words subsided and she stopped to catch her breath.

"My, you've been through a lot!" Sonia said. "You're incredibly patient and persistent. You need to accept that working with multiple cultures is a skillset that requires steady growth over time. When I first started out, I was as monocultural as you are. I learned by making lots of mistakes and trying to not repeat them.

Sometimes I come to the place where I believe I understand a partner's thinking. Then we have a surprising conversation and I say to myself, 'What just happened?' Because many of our global partners are extremely polite, I'm never absolutely certain whether my actions are inoffensive or my training materials are helpful.

The longer you do this, the better you will become at it. But it never becomes systematic and orderly, like an assembly line. The most common word I hear people use to describe cross-cultural partnerships is *messy*. That's because we're dealing with people, and people are messy."

Susan frowned. "But Brad and Jennifer Nelson know Japanese culture so deeply. They're fluent in the language, understand cultural nuances, and get Japanese to laugh in ways I never will."

"That's not a fair comparison," Sonia said. "The Nelsons are full-time missionaries who attended two years of language school and have lived among the Japanese people for over ten years. That's not what you're calling the people of Fragrant Hills to do.

I like to think of the difference between a submarine and a harbor. A submarine goes underwater for months at a time without coming up for air or food. That's what the Nelsons do. They lay aside their American way of doing things. In Japan they speak Japanese, eat with chopsticks, and ride the crowded subways. But the way they love Japanese in America is to help them learn English, eat with a knife and fork, and drive a car. That's what a harbor does. A harbor never goes underwater. Instead, it stands on the shoreline inviting ships of different nationalities to dock so their passengers can disembark safely on dry land."

"I like that analogy," said Susan. "I believe the people of Fragrant Hills will resonate with the concept of being a safe harbor that welcomes people of many nationalities as they adjust to life in the U.S. We wouldn't expect staff at the harbor coffee shop to speak multiple languages or accept multiple currencies. Their job is simply to extend a warm welcome to everyone who comes ashore."

"That's right," said Sonia. "I don't encourage American Christians who befriend immigrants to think of themselves as missionaries. I prefer to think of them as Connectors. They help connect newcomers to the systems and resources they need to adapt to life in America. A personal relationship with an insider is one of the most valuable resources a newcomer can have."

Susan nodded. "That's a really helpful perspective. Thanks for sharing it. Let me raise another concern. I feel very isolated and alone here in Columbus. Pastor Jeremy is supportive, but I know how he functions. He's an effective delegator who chooses highly talented staff and volunteers, then empowers them to do their ministries with minimal supervision or support. I know I have his full backing. But he is not going to be with me in the trenches with his sleeves rolled up. Whatever I learn, I have to figure out on my own."

Sonia took a sip of her masala tea. "From what I'm seeing, that's not unusual for senior pastors. I've met a few

American pastors who are wonderfully cross-culturally gifted. Other churches have no one in the congregation with strong cross-cultural skills. And then there are churches such as Fragrant Hills that have someone like you who is learning cross-cultural skills."

"Everyone in the church is so busy," Susan said. "If there are programs that need to be launched, I am going to need to launch them myself. Pastor Jeremy has made it very clear that other than an occasional meeting, he has little time to dedicate to me. And the members of our church are each engaged in two, three, or four different kinds of ministry, and get stressed out when I suggest adding anything else to their plates."

"That sounds typical as well." Sonia leaned back in her chair. "We need to find ways for churches to engage in cross-cultural ministry that don't necessarily place huge demands on the time and energy of the staff and laypeople."

Susan tapped on the table in thought. "Busyness isn't the only issue. Often, it's plain disinterest. When I share with many of the people at Fragrant Hills and others in the Great Lakes district about the wonderful, godly people that God has brought from around the world to the U.S., they look at me politely but blankly, with an expression that says, 'That's very nice, but I really don't care.' The majority of people in our district churches seem apathetic at best.

And it's not just the Americans. When I speak with the pastors of our partnering Latino, Vietnamese, and South Sudanese congregations, they all tell me they themselves value partnership with American pastors, but most of the people in their congregation don't see the point. They don't feel welcome in American culture, struggle to speak English, and see Sunday morning as an opportunity to retreat into their native language and culture. Their service is like an oasis to retreat into the kinds of worship they enjoyed in their homelands. So it seems like, whether I'm talking to American or immigrant Christians, most people really aren't interested in working together."

"Susan, you just described Miramar Hindi Fellowship. Our people just want to retreat into our clannish Indian community on Sunday. American and immigrant churches both need to realize if we don't engage in cross-cultural ministry, our churches are headed for extinction. Our first-generation churches that do not win the hearts of our children and grandchildren in English will only last for one generation.

And most American churches are graying and in decline. We know the denominations that serve alongside immigrant ministry leaders have higher membership retention rates than those that don't."

"I know," Susan said. "Yet even faced with our own extinction, it's hard to gain traction motivating people to want to change the status quo."

"You're absolutely correct," said Sonia. "We have a few solid partnerships serving as role models. Yet it's really hard to gain traction with most of our districts. My HR directors are motivated to develop cross-cultural skills because they report to me. They know they won't keep their jobs if their teams keep falling apart. But pastors have no such incentive. We need to identify the keys that will motivate them to desire cross-cultural partnerships. Having success stories to tell is a strong first step forward. We need to keep forming more healthy partnerships, expanding the ones we have, and sharing their stories across the denomination. Most of all, we need to join in united prayer that God will stir the hearts of His people to desire to serve alongside their global brothers and sisters."

"Amen!" Susan replied. "When I hear the South Sudanese and Latinos pray, it's like they have a direct line to the throne of grace that we're lacking." She perked up. "Oh, I just thought of something I need to ask you. I had an embarrassing moment last week. When I told a friend that I was thrilled to have an Indian mentor, she asked, 'That's wonderful! Is your mentor Mohawk, Navajo, or something else?' I never thought of that. What exactly should I call you?"

"I get asked that all the time," Sonia said. "In international business, finding terminology that satisfies everyone is not easy. When I'm in a meeting and I'm reasonably sure no Native Americans are present, I simply refer to myself as an Indian. But in other contexts, I refer to myself as an Asian Indian.

That's only one example. In San Diego, I rarely use the term 'black.' African Americans and African immigrants are so distinct that they often don't want to be mistaken for each other. So I choose words that distinguish the two.

If there are no Latinos in a meeting, I refer to Guatemalans as Guatemalans, Mexicans as Mexicans, and people from the United States as Americans. However, peoples from every country in North, Central, and South America rightfully regard themselves as Americans. So if there are Latinos in a meeting with staff from Europe and the United States, I open by expressing that I acknowledge all peoples from the Western Hemisphere as Americans, but in our meeting I will use the term American to refer exclusively to people from the United States.

And I have to be careful about national borders, too. If one of our staff refers to Taiwan as its own country, we could lose all our business in China."

Susan's eyes bulged. "Wow, that's a lot to keep track of."

"And that's just about nationalities," Sonia said. "It's also true about generations. My daughter Anushka doesn't like being referred to as a second-generation immigrant. She says, 'Mom, I was born here! I'm one hundred percent as American as everybody else!' And she's right. Yet she ticks every box sociologists use to describe a second-generation immigrant.

And today we need to consider whether some in a meeting would like everyone to express their preferred gender pronouns."

"Ugh!" said Susan. "This much complexity makes my brain hurt! I realize you do this for a living. But the pastors and laypeople of Parkerite churches don't. If we're going to require them to get all this vocabulary straight before they can love people from other countries, they will get discouraged and give up."

"You're right," Sonia said. "The greater the complexity of languages, nationalities, ethnicities and generations in a conversation, the harder it will be to find terminology that satisfies everyone."

"So what do we do?" Susan asked. "Be content with offending people? What do you teach your HR managers?"

Sonia replied, "I have a very clear protocol for training new HR directors in a multicultural context. They need to know the specific audiences they will be addressing. Depending on the clients they serve, they may never need to distinguish Asian Indians from Native Americans, African Americans from African immigrants in America, or Mexicans from Americans. But they may need to resolve local ethnic issues.

I ask them to try choosing terminology appropriate for their audience. But in a culturally complex setting, it's inevitable someone will be displeased with the language that is used. A few will give us feedback, but most will remain silently disappointed.

And I've found that different people from the same background will prefer different terminology. It's simply impossible to use everyone's preferred terminology."

Susan threw her hands up. "You need a Ph.D. to figure all of this out! It's unrealistic to expect laypeople and even pastors to know all this. What are a group of monocultural white Parkerites supposed to do?"

"Exactly the same thing a bunch of monocultural Indians— oops, I meant to say Asian Indians--in San Diego do," Sonia replied. "We do our sincere best to use inoffensive language. If someone tells us they prefer different terminology, we try to change. But it's inevitable some will feel excluded by our choice of words, but say nothing. This is part of the reality of working with people across languages, cultures, and generations."

Susan paused for a deep breath. "This is going to take a while to sink in."

"Let me bring up another subject," Sonia said. "I want to ask you about one of the current trends in cross-cultural ministry today. A number of monocultural churches are making the transition to multicultural churches. I know you've seen it there in Columbus."

"Yes," Susan said. "A few years back, Pleasant Valley Church transitioned from monocultural to multicultural. I've worshipped there and enjoy their spirit. It really feels like Revelation chapter five, where all the nations, tribes, tongues, and people come together in worship before the throne of God. It's a beautiful expression of worship.

But it hasn't been easy. Pleasant Valley lost a lot of members in the transition who left for other monocultural churches. Fragrant Hills picked up a few of them. Pastor Anderson makes it very clear that it is difficult for him to maintain leadership teams, and even Sunday morning attendance, as they navigate different sets of cultural expectations."

"Yes," Sonia agreed. "Multicultural churches may be a big part of our future, but they are not a one-size-fits-all solution. There are certain kinds of people who are naturally attracted to them, but we need to accept that most people aren't.

As we encourage multicultural ministry across the Parkerite Church, there are three primary models we're looking at. The first is transitioning existing monocultural churches to multicultural. Now Susan, what do you think would happen if Pastor Jeremy suggested that Fragrant Hills go multicultural?"

"Civil war!" Susan blurted out. Then she paused to express something a bit more diplomatic. "Well, likely a major split, or at least a slow bleed."

Sonia laughed. "Most people prefer worshiping with others like themselves, and many of them will leave if a church transitions to multicultural worship. That's why a second model we're exploring is leaving a church's monocultural worship service intact while launching a second multicultural expression of worship. It could be a small group, a second worship service, or even a daughter church."

"That makes sense." Susan agreed, "Because it would leave the first group intact for those who prefer it, and also allow for the creation of a new group. This sounds like the model we're all familiar with, where churches have both traditional and contemporary services. And it's possible the second group might someday become larger than the first one."

"The third option we're exploring," Sonia said, "Is to do what you're doing at Fragrant Hills, which is for an existing American church to partner with monocultural immigrant churches in the community. In most cases, the relationship progresses no further than the mere sharing of space. I call these churches 'religious roommates.' But what you and Pastor Jeremy are doing is building personal relationships and ministry partnerships with these pastors. That's a model we would love to see expanded across Parkerites nationwide."

"That's our goal," said Susan. "But the progress is a lot slower than I'd like."

Sonia said, "Dr. Peter Nnadi is Director of the Master's program in Cross-Cultural Ministry at Parker Seminary. Have you considered enrolling?"

Susan shook her head. "When I talk to people who teach cross-cultural skills, it's like they assume I'm going to quit my job and move to the mission field. They expect me to read reams of books about sociology, anthropology, and linguistics. They use buzzwords that everyday people don't use, like 'diaspora,' 'majority world,' 'ethnocentricity,' 'minority culture,' and 'power distance.' If Pastor Jeremy started talking like that from the pulpit, people would not respond well.

It feels to me like training on cross-cultural skills is aimed at those who want to dive into the deep end of the culture learning pool. I have a church full of people who might be willing to stick their toe in the pool. If it's not too cold, they might stick their foot in. And I hope that someday they'll finally jump in. But Sonia, we've got to find some kind of cross-cultural training that's wired for everyday people who aren't going to use insider jargon or spend lots of time reading."

Sonia smiled. "We need both kinds of training in the corporate world as well. I require all my HR directors to take mandatory classes in cross-cultural awareness and to spend time understanding the cultures of any new region they are assigned. They become quite articulate about the cultural differences between their team members.

But part of their job is to instill cross-cultural sensitivity into the programmers, project managers, sales reps, admins, and others that make up their teams. Many of these come from monocultural offices where they can dedicate all their energies to their technical expertise without thinking about cross-cultural communication. In theory I would love to see each HR director or team lead write up some sort of simple cross-cultural guide specific to their team. But you know how busy our team members are, and at this point such documentation is only wishful thinking.

I resonate with what you're telling me, Susan. We need Christian leaders who take advanced intercultural training at places like Parker. But they need to understand they are outliers and shouldn't expect the average pastor to reach their level of competence. I'd hope that some of them will write materials appropriate for everyday believers. Maybe we could call it 'Intercultural Skills 101'."

"Yeah, I think we'd find ourselves in a lawsuit if we tried using a trademarked name like 'Cultural Skills for Dummies'," Susan said.

Sonia concluded their conversation by saying, "Susan, I just want to affirm you. You're doing a fine job. I can see clearly you've grown so much in the past few months. Ultimately, you and I are doing exactly the same thing. We build relationships. We make a lot of mistakes, but the mistakes aren't bad enough to end relationships. We keep learning by what we read and by the people we meet. I am absolutely confident that as you and I continue to talk, I will see the ongoing development of your ministry skills."

Sonia's mentoring and affirmation gave Susan confidence that she was on the right track and would gradually develop her intercultural skills over time.

***

Let me interrupt the narrative of Susan's story at this point. I created Susan as a composite of American pastoral leaders I have encountered through the years. I hope you will identify with parts of her journey.

In the next chapter, I want to share my own journey with you. The pastors and churches you will read about in Susan's narrative are composites of those I've experienced. But my story will include real-world examples of pastors and churches that are helpful role models.

4

Realities from Beijing to
Minneapolis

M y journey of equipping ministry leaders to cultivate
cross-cultural church partnerships began with
pastoring at an international church in Beijing, China.
Sherry and I moved to Beijing in 2006 after completing two
years of Mandarin language study in neighboring Tianjin.
During our 11 years in Beijing, we fell in love with Chinese
people, food, language, and culture.

During those years, I was one of the pastors of the Beijing
International Christian Fellowship. The Chinese government
doesn't issue many permits for foreign churches. Our elders
received a license to host one large Protestant church. We
were not permitted to enter a relationship with any foreign
denomination. We told our members, "When you worship
here, you're not a Baptist, a Lutheran or a Pentecostal.
You're a Christian. You're not a Nigerian, a Brazilian or an
American. You're a Christian. Christians are the only kind
of people that enter heaven, anyway. So let's all worship,
learn, and fellowship together as Christians."

Our church consisted of 3,000 people from 70 nations. We
held services in 11 languages. Our English-language

congregation looked like the United Nations. About half were Asian, a quarter were African, and most of the rest were Caucasian. Many spoke English as their second, third, or fourth languages. Once per quarter, the 11 different language congregations came together for Unity Sunday, in which different groups led worship, prayer, and teaching. These gatherings felt like the vision of worship prophesied in Revelation chapters 5 and 7, where all nations, tribes, tongues, and people come together to worship before the throne of God. It was an unforgettable experience!

Our pulpit rotation team and elder board consisted of pastors from several denominations and ethnicities. Every Wednesday morning, our pastors came together for mutual encouragement, prayer, and training. Some were full-time staff members. Some were missionaries with other responsibilities who committed part of their time to the church. Others had secular jobs and volunteered their time as well. We made theological education and counseling training available to all who needed them.

Although we came from different parts of the world, these brothers made a diligent, dedicated effort to love, support, and pray for one another. In that setting, I learned the different needs of pastors from diverse cultural, linguistic, and denominational backgrounds.

During those years I traveled to 17 Asian countries, training ministry leaders in church planting and pastoral theology. In country after country, I met wonderfully gifted servants of God. They were as diverse as you can imagine. Some had Ph.D.'s and others were illiterate. Some were wealthy; others lived in communities without electricity or plumbing. Some enjoyed political and religious freedom while others experienced significant oppression.

What made them remarkable was not their differences, but their commonalities. They were all committed to the Word of God as truth. They loved sharing the gospel, nurturing believers, and planting new churches. They had prayer habits that eclipse those of us in the Western church. That doesn't mean I'm naively optimistic about them. Each of these leaders are sinners who struggle with spiritual health like everyone else. Yet I've been greatly impressed by the devout faith and ministry giftedness of many of these Asian ministry leaders. What this knowledge says to me is that many Asian ministry leaders who emigrate to the U.S. are highly gifted servants of God. After returning to the U.S., I discovered the same is true for ministry leaders who have immigrated from other parts of the world as well.

When Sherry and I returned to Minnesota in 2017, we entered an extended period of prayer, reflection, and dialogue about the future of our ministry. One of our supporting churches, Westwood Church of Chanhassen, was launching a 10-year ministry initiative of planting and strengthening immigrant churches in the community. They asked if I would consider providing 25% of my time as their consultant, serving as boots on the ground to build relationships with pastors in our local immigrant communities. I served happily in that role for three years.

Since then, I have worshiped in more than 80 immigrant churches in the Minneapolis area. As I chose the churches I visited, I alternated among ethnicities, denominations, and sizes, wanting to experience the breadth of the local body of Christ. I knew I had awareness of the Asian context but was an outsider to African and Latino cultures.

I wondered if Africans and Latinos would like me. My personality is much like that of my Chinese friends—quiet, soft-spoken, and not particularly huggy or emotionally expressive. Stereotypically, Latinos and Africans are known to be loud, emotional, and huggy—everything I'm not. I wondered if I would be well-received by pastors in these communities.

When I visited churches, I declined any opportunity to preach. I notified the pastor in advance of my visit, stating I had come to hear him share the Word of God. Whenever possible, I would invite that pastor to lunch, or dinner, or tea later. I developed a set of useful questions that conveyed sincere interest in their lives:

- What was it like growing up in your homeland?
- How did you come to America?
- How did you start your church?
- How are your kids doing in school?
- What's difficult about living in the U.S.?
- What's difficult about pastoring in the U.S.?
- If an American church were to minister alongside you, what would that look like?

After every conversation, each of those pastors felt loved, heard, validated, and affirmed. Even though my personality is quite different from theirs, they liked me! That's something I've observed to be universal. Anyone who can lay aside their own interests and show genuine interest in the story of the person they're speaking with can build a trusting relationship with them.

As I continued to understand the lives of diverse immigrant pastors, I also spoke with many American pastors about their relationships with immigrant churches. Many American churches host immigrant churches in their facilities, but their relationships proceed no further than the mere sharing of space. I refer to these as "religious roommates." The sharing of space in itself is a commendable ministry, but it comes short of providing the churches with the benefits of relational and ministry partnerships.

I've seen churches that have moved beyond the sharing of space into also sharing some level of joint ministry. The types of shared ministries are numerous, such as concerts, outreach events, community service, or children's and youth ministries. Inevitably, tensions will arise when Christians of different cultural backgrounds serve together. Most pastors view their partnerships from a task-focused perspective instead of a relationally-focused perspective. In such cases, communication is infrequent, disillusionment is common, and misunderstandings go unaddressed.

A smaller number of churches have made the effort to develop robust partnerships. I will share some of their stories in Chapter 6.

As I spoke with pastors about cross-cultural church partnerships, they said, "John, nobody else is talking about this." As a result, in 2019, I founded Immigrant Ministry Connections, and launched its website www.immigrantministry.com. Our mission is to create a vibrant future for American Christianity by equipping American and immigrant believers and churches to serve together in cross-cultural and cross-generational ministry.

Our resources have increased over time. We began by posting weekly blogs. Later we added online directories of nonprofit ministry organizations in all 50 states and all 13 provinces and territories of Canada. These directories include websites with Bibles in more than 4,000 languages and disciple-making videos in hundreds of languages. Later, we added digital courses to our online offerings.

In the fall of 2023, I began coaching online cohorts through The Merging Streams Coalition (www.immigrantministry.com/mergingstreams). The name of our Coalition refers to American churches, first-generation immigrant churches, and second-plus-generation immigrant churches that are inevitably merging to form the new face of American Christianity.

Prior to the launch of The Merging Streams Coalition, I had been consulting with individual pastors for quite some time, enjoying one-on-one conversations. Our small group cohorts have brought together denominational leaders and pastors from diverse ethnicities, locations, and denominations. All of us process one key question:

How can we multiply healthy cross-cultural church partnerships between two churches or across an entire district or denomination?

These cohorts have led to high degrees of synergy and cooperation across the Body of Christ.

One of the key issues that emerged during our discussions was the need for a brief, simple overview of the steps necessary to motivate believers to desire and launch healthy cross-cultural church partnerships. This book was written in response to that need. My hope is that you will be better equipped to build peer relationships with diverse pastors in your community because of what I've written.

In Chapters 6-8, I will provide you with a Quick Start Guide for launching healthy cross-cultural church partnerships. To properly set the stage, let's rejoin Susan Jamison for an important lesson about communication.

5

Defining the Problem

Susan and her friend Janet Griswold seated themselves at The Green Scene—their favorite lunch spot to treat themselves after a tennis match. The two had been tennis partners at Ohio State. Because Janet's family was also part of Fragrant Hills Church, the two of them maintained their friendship over the years. Weekly tennis matches kept them accountable for a healthy lifestyle. So did lunch at The Green Scene.

The two of them caught up on the latest about their husbands, children, and jobs. That led naturally to a conversation about Susan's position as Multicultural Partnership Catalyst. By now, Susan had been in her new role for six months. She told Janet how much she loved having Sonia as a mentor. But both women continued to struggle to gain significant momentum in cultivating cross-cultural church partnerships.

Susan had developed strong traction at the local level. Some of the youth from Fragrant Hills' partnering Vietnamese and South Sudanese churches had joined their Wednesday night youth group.

Fragrant Hills' part-time youth pastor, Shane, had developed good working relationships with the Vietnamese and South Sudanese volunteer youth pastors. Their youth had fun together, the adult volunteers were building relationships, and it seemed like a solid win for all three congregations. Pastor Jeremy affirmed Susan for the excellent work she was doing.

But mobilizing other churches to partner cross-culturally remained a grind. She had spoken at conferences and in individual churches. Pastors would listen to her politely, but the blank stares in their eyes betrayed their disinterest. They would offer appreciation with phrases like "God bless you for serving in this vital ministry." But it was obvious they had no passion to engage immigrant believers in their communities.

One pastor from Dayton felt overwhelmed by his current workload. He said, "My people come to me with visions of new ministries I need to launch that would add to my workload. I've been approached about launching a marriage ministry, a recovery ministry, a singles ministry, and more. And now you're telling me I need to start an immigrant ministry. I feel guilty for not launching every kind of good ministry people want me to do."

Susan had not expected so many pastors to respond this way. Even at Fragrant Hills, where members had seen obvious results from their cross-cultural partnerships, Susan struggled to build momentum towards expanding cross-cultural relationships.

Janet replied, "Why on earth would a group of white people, who have spent their entire lives fellowshipping with other white people, want to befriend Latinos? And why would a group of Latinos, with their own unique culture and language, want to befriend a bunch of Anglos?"

Susan flinched. She expected indifference, but this direct approach raised her defensive hackles.

Janet smiled in sympathy. "Susan, I believe in what you're doing. I believe in you. And I want to see you multiply cross-cultural partnerships at Fragrant Hills and across the district. But you own this vision so deeply that you're too close to it. When you speak to people, you assume they will love it as much as you do. You need to understand that people haven't walked in your shoes and can't relate to your experiences."

Relaxing slightly, Susan realized Janet wasn't being adversarial. She just wanted to help her view things from a different perspective.

Janet leaned in. "So why don't most Americans want cross-cultural partnerships?"

Susan had to stop and think about that for a moment. When she reflected on the history of Fragrant Hills, it became very clear.

"It's because Fragrant Hills is composed of white people who learned the Bible from other white people, shared the gospel with other white people, and built churches full of white people. And you can trace this all the way back to the Great Awakening. The heroes of American Christianity we revere are Jonathan Edwards, George Whitefield, D. L. Moody, and Billy Graham, who are people who look like us. We have centuries of history of white people winning other white people to Christ, and thus expanding the Kingdom of God. Viewing people of other ethnicities as spiritual leaders who can transform American Christianity is a foreign concept to us. Why would Americans want to change something that has been working for centuries?"

"That sounds about right," Janet said. "So now let me ask, 'Why don't most immigrant Christians want partnerships with Americans?'"

Not being an insider to their cultures, Susan had to think a bit longer about that one. But finally, she said, "These people learned how to love the Lord in their homelands. They grew up in Caracas, Juba, and Saigon, and that's where other Christians taught them how to pray, study the Bible, make disciples, and plant churches. And now that they're in Columbus, they're replicating precisely what they did in their homelands. What they did in their homelands never necessitated partnering with any other ethnicities. They're simply doing what has always worked."

"Precisely!" said Janet. "Now we're onto something! Both sides keep doing what they're doing because they've always known it, because it worked in the past, and because they love it. It's their tradition. So the next question is, 'Why aren't those practices still working?'"

Susan found that a lot easier to answer. From the immigrant side, the answer was obvious. "They're not in their homelands anymore. While their methods are effective at making disciples of fellow first-generation immigrants, they are far less effective at reaching the hearts of their own children. Their children speak English, think like Westerners, and aren't attracted to the worship of their parents' churches.

On the American side, it's not quite as obvious. For centuries, America was primarily white. But over the last thirty or forty years, America has become increasingly multicultural. Many Gen Z high schools no longer have any majority group. Young generations of Americans are used to functioning in a multicultural society. A church that only knows how to work with whites or Mexicans or Chinese or

Russians is going to ultimately become ineffective in our multicultural society."

Susan paused for a moment, realizing that neither side had much incentive to change the status quo. She said, "Over the decades, people have learned styles of preaching, worship, and prayer that they deeply love. They will always lobby their pastors to keep providing those kinds of services. If their pastors try to change those services, their people will push back, and in many cases leave. So there's a lot of pressure to keep churches the way they've always been."

Janet nodded encouragingly. "Now you've identified why people keep doing things the way they've always done them. And you've identified why those things don't work anymore. The next question is, 'What motivates people to change? Why would Christians want to start engaging in the kinds of ministries that you're proposing?'"

Susan stammered in her response. "Umm… because they love Jesus? And the Great Commission? And the unity of the body of Christ?"

Janet said, "That's a good start. But those things have been true for two thousand years, and pastors are still looking back at you with blank stares. What would it take for them to *want* to change?"

Susan held her hands out. "I don't know. Please help me, Janet. What really motivates people to change?"

Janet raised a single finger: "Pain."

At Susan's confused look, she continued.

"People change to avoid pain. People don't enjoy getting colonoscopies, mammograms, and prostate exams. But they get them because their friends have had cancer. People fasten their seatbelts, buy life insurance, and see therapists because they dislike pain. If you want to promote this ministry, you're going to have to help people get in touch with their pain.

So let me ask you, 'What is the pain that the people of Fragrant Hills and the pastors of the Great Lakes District face that would make them willing to change the status quo?'"

"Pain?" Susan stared at her half-eaten salad in thought. "The biggest pain I can identify is that the American church is in decline, and we don't know what to do about it." After another moment, she added, "The American church isn't prepared to thrive in a multicultural society, and we don't know what to do about that either."

"Excellent," said Janet, "And what is the pain point for the immigrant church?"

The answer leapt to Susan's lips. "They don't know how to disciple their children in a way that keeps them in church as adults."

"Spot on!" said Janet. "From what I can see, you're learning to clearly articulate the pain that will motivate Christians to desire change. The next question is whether you have something that will actually address that pain. Are you a snake oil salesperson, or can you produce genuine results?

"What we have seen in our Wednesday evening youth group has been transformative," Susan said. "We've got youth from three different ethnicities learning together. We've got volunteer laborers from three different cultures serving as a united team. And the students are having fun. They're making friendships. They're messaging each other on social media and getting together at school. We've been able to connect youth with resources to help them cope with issues like drugs and pornography and finishing high school.

Some of these young people who graduated from youth group are remaining in church. Some of them are staying in their parents' churches, and others are coming to the English service at Fragrant Hills with their parents' full knowledge and consent. It seems like we really have proof that cross-cultural partnerships address the pain both sides are experiencing."

Then Susan realized that wasn't always the case. "But not for everyone. I helped Nathan Road Church in Indianapolis partner with a Kenyan congregation. Nathan Road had its glory days in the 1950s, but today it has an average attendance of twenty-two white people whose average age is seventy-one. They know their church probably won't be around for very long. Then the Kenyans came in. There are thirty-five of them. They have a church of young couples with lots of babies, large families. They're making disciples and the church is growing. But Nathan Road is still in decline."

Janet said, "So what you're telling me is that this doesn't always result in church growth."

"That's right."

"But does it still result in Kingdom growth?"

"That's a great question. I'll have to think about that." Susan took another bite of kale and measured her response as she chewed. "Certainly, we're all passionate about the Great Commission. But that's not the only measure of obedience. We must also remain passionate about the unity of the Body of Christ. Even if none of the churches in a partnership grow numerically, they're still being obedient in answering Jesus' prayer 'That they may all be one.' And that makes them more attractive to the non-Christian members of the community."

Susan sat up straighter, feeling more energized. "You're really onto something here, Janet. But what about the pastor from Dayton who was overwhelmed with his workload and couldn't take on a new immigrant ministry? What would I say to someone like him?"

"Now you're talking about **how** and **what** issues," Janet said. "But avoiding pain is a **why** issue. If you convince people about the **why**—if they've identified a pain point and believe you can address it, they will figure out how to address **what** and **how** issues. Now, did it take a lot of time, energy, or expense for you to adapt your youth group to effectively serve three different congregations?"

"No, it really didn't cost anything. It took very little of Pastor Jeremy's time. He empowered Pastor Shane to build relationships with the two volunteer youth leaders from the other groups. Shane made sure that Fragrant Hills' volunteers understood some of the differences they would face. For instance, not all cultures place equal value on starting or ending events at a given time. But other than that, it has taken little time or energy to retrofit our youth ministry to suit these three churches."

"That's a great start. That story alone tells me there are things an American church can do without a massive commitment of time, energy, and finances that will minister to the needs of their partnering immigrant congregations."

Susan was delighted as Janet helped her articulate the real issues. At the same time, the task still loomed large and overwhelming.

"Janet, let me restate what I hear you saying. You're telling me this: *All I need to do* is communicate to American and immigrant pastors and laypeople that they have a problem that needs to be fixed; that cross-cultural church partnerships can address those problems; that those partnerships can be implemented without a massive investment of time, energy, and finances; and can be kept healthy for the long-term."

"Yes, that sounds about right."

Susan couldn't help the snort that escaped her. "Okay, so that's *all* I need to do? That's a massive project! You're almost telling me I'm going to have to write a book."

Janet made a *slow down* motion. "Sometimes what we need are short, practical, how-to guides. Two months ago, I bought a new laptop. When I opened the box, on top was a Quick Start Guide with a series of pictures that showed me how to plug it in, turn it on, power it up, and begin to use it. Now, I know that fully understanding the features of my new laptop would require a thick manual. But that Quick Start Guide was enough to get me started.

Susan, I know that over the past six months you've been learning reams about cross-cultural ministry. But is there any way that you can boil down that knowledge into sort of a 'Quick Start Guide' for cross-cultural church partnerships?"

"Maybe you're right," Susan said. "It feels like these ideas I've learned are constantly swirling around in my head. And I'm trying to make everyone learn all of it. Maybe I do need to write something. I'll need to check with Sonia and get her approval first."

Janet smiled. "Don't worry about the writing part. I'm a communications major. My specialty is helping people take abstract concepts and restating them in words that are understandable and persuasive. If you help me understand the core of what you are trying to communicate, I can help you refine your words in a way that the people of Fragrant Hills will find compelling.

Oh, and be sure to tell stories. You know a lot of abstract concepts about cross-cultural skills. People will be better able to grasp your abstract concepts if you wrap them around relatable stories."

Susan left that meeting with gratitude and confidence. It felt like a significant step toward motivating pastoral leaders to desire and implement cross-cultural church partnerships.

━━━

That is exactly what I want to share with you over the next three chapters. Temporarily laying aside Susan's narrative, the next three chapters comprise a Quick Start Guide, explaining in clear terms how to convince American and immigrant pastors and laypeople why we have a problem that needs to be addressed; how cross-cultural church partnerships can address those problems; how those partnerships can be implemented without massive outlays of time, energy, and money; and how they can remain healthy for the long term.

When a new family from out of state moves into your neighborhood, you don't necessarily need to be reconciled to them. First and foremost, you need to welcome them. The message of this book is *welcome*, not *reconciliation*. Many popular books written from various perspectives address issues of reconciliation between races that have lived in America for multiple generations. Addressing those issues here would multiply the length and complexity of this book. In these pages, I simply invite those of all backgrounds whose families have lived here for centuries to focus on obeying God's mandate for citizens of any country to welcome the newcomers living among us.

6

Quick Start Guideline 1: Cast a Compelling Vision

The next three chapters will cover three guidelines for launching healthy partnerships between American and immigrant churches. These guidelines address the questions of **why**, **who**, **what**, and **how** that form the indispensable elements of a healthy partnership. We'll start with **why**. Answering this question will create motivation for others to join you on the journey. In the next chapter, I'll address **who**, enumerating the kinds of people necessary to form a healthy partnership. And in the third chapter, I'll address the tactile questions of **what** and **how** that are necessary for a successful launch event.

As Susan and Janet discussed in Chapter 5, most of us would rather build partnerships with other people like us. It takes powerful motivations to change these innate preferences. Asking **why** touches us at the deepest level of our hearts. Those whose hearts align with yours on the **why** question will have the motivation to serve alongside you to address **who**, **what**, and **how**.

For all you teachers out there, I've organized in this chapter around a 3-point outline for clear presentation:

Three Reasons All American and Immigrant Churches Need Partnerships

1. The Bible commands it.
2. Thriving in a multicultural society requires it.
3. Ordinary churches are successfully doing it.

1. The Bible Commands It

Let's examine four biblical passages exhorting believers to love those from other cultures.

Acts 1:8 "You will receive power when the Holy Spirit has come upon you, and you will be my witnesses in Jerusalem, and in all Judea and Samaria, and to the end of the earth."

Judea was the home of the Jews, and it represents those around us who are like us. Neighboring Samaria was "the wrong side of the tracks," and it represents those around us who aren't like us. Jesus wants us to love all peoples, whether they live near us or on the other side of the world.

Many Christians only regard serving other ethnicities as 'missions' if those people live overseas. They will give generously to serve Nepalis in Nepal. But when Nepalis move to their own neighborhoods, suddenly those same Christians aren't quite as ready to be generous.

Additionally, when Nepalis are in Nepal, we must send someone else to serve them. If they live nearby, suddenly *we* can serve them. That makes us uncomfortable, because most of us aren't really interested in serving them ourselves. But Jesus' command is to love all peoples who live in Judea and Samaria as well as in the remotest parts of the earth.

Sharing Christ locally as well as globally is indispensable to the Great Commission.

Leviticus 19:33-34 "When a stranger sojourns with you in your land, you shall not do him wrong. You shall treat the stranger who sojourns with you as the native among you. You shall love him as yourself, for you were strangers in the land of Egypt. I am the LORD your God."

God spoke these words just months after the people had crossed the Red Sea, camping at the foot of Mount Sinai. They had vivid memories of the atrocities they had suffered as foreigners in Egypt. God commanded that when they entered the Promised Land, enjoying its milk and honey, they should remember the oppression they experienced as foreigners. Those memories should remind them to treat foreigners living among them in the Promised Land with great kindness.

When Jesus was asked which is the greatest commandment in the Law, he replied "to love God with all your heart, soul, mind, and strength." He added that the second greatest commandment is the one we just read. Notice the subject Moses is discussing: how to treat foreigners. Jesus' point is that Christians of any country are responsible to treat the native-born and the foreign-born with equal compassion.

1 Corinthians 12:21 "The eye cannot say to the hand, 'I have no need of you,' nor again the head to the feet, 'I have no need of you.'"

America's culture is the world's most individualistic. It's difficult enough for us to accept that we need partnership with others like ourselves, let alone those who are different from us. But Paul makes it clear that no member of the body of Christ can say to any other member, "I don't need you."

Building cross-cultural church partnerships is one of the best ways to share our spiritual gifts with one another. Such cross-cultural relationships can serve as powerful testimonies to racially divided communities. They also serve as a foretaste of the gathering of believers from all ethnicities before the throne of God, as prophesied in Revelation chapters 5 and 7.

Romans 15:7 "Therefore welcome one another as Christ has welcomed you, for the glory of God."

Why did Christ welcome us? Because we were worthy? Because we had money or something else God needed? Absolutely not! The only basis any of us have to enter heaven is the mercy of God. Because of this, we have no ground to reject others because we dislike the color of their skin, their citizenship status, their language, or their style of worship. When we kneel at the foot of the cross, the ground is level and we must receive one another as peers.

2. Thriving in a Multicultural Society Requires It

Biblical commands alone should be enough to compel Christians to pursue multicultural partnerships. But there are compelling contemporary reasons as well.

In Chapter 5, Janet told Susan people aren't motivated to change until they're in touch with pain. Christians who don't feel that pain will regard cross-cultural partnerships as a "nice" ministry that isn't essential to the future of the church. Those who have an acute sense of that pain will prioritize cross-cultural partnerships on the church's calendar and budget. In Chapter 5, Janet articulated three pain points for American and immigrant churches:

1. The American church is in decline.
2. First-generation immigrant churches are failing to retain most of their children.
3. Neither American nor first-generation immigrant churches are prepared to thrive in a multicultural society.

It's easy to find fault with the church. It's much harder to propose solutions that address these deficiencies. Let me share four positive impacts of cross-cultural partnerships that address these pain points.

Positive Impact #1: First-generation immigrant Christians have innate qualities that strengthen American Christianity.

In today's polarized climate regarding immigration policy, it's difficult for many American Christians to see any positive value in immigration. The Bible does not provide definitive governmental immigration policies, and obedient Christians can hold different opinions on the issue. However, we must not allow our differences at the *policy* level to override our responsibility at the *personal* level to "Do unto others as you would have them do unto you."

Having worshipped in over 80 churches of immigrant believers, here are some positive qualities I've generally observed.

- *Youth.* On the whole, the members of immigrant churches are younger than members of American churches. In many cases, it's at least a full generation younger!

- *Higher birth rates.* Americans in general, including Christians, have comparatively low birth rates. Latino and African Christians who emigrate to America typically have higher birth rates[1], meaning that more children growing up in the U.S. are being raised in the faith.
- *Momentum.* Many Christian immigrants to North America come from countries where the church has experienced sustained growth and expect that growth to continue.
- *Theological and moral conservatism.* Most immigrant pastors I've met are expressly clear they do not desire partnerships with churches holding to progressive views on theology and morality.
- *A strong sense of community.* America's trend toward individualism has been intensified by the pandemic and our ideological polarization. Our immigrant communities remind us of the social, emotional, and spiritual benefits of belonging to community.
- *An unshakable belief that God's supernatural power impacts our daily lives.* While some Western theologians question the reality of miracles, I've not yet met anyone in the immigrant community with such reservations. Global Christians don't believe in miracles simply because of the Bible schools they attended, but because they are convinced they've experienced them in their daily lives.

Those are my personal observations. There is also national research providing encouragement about the positive impact of immigrant believers on American Christianity. In 2022, Lifeway conducted a survey of hundreds of Latino churches in several denominations across the U.S.[2] Here are some of its findings:

- Over half of these churches were young, having been planted in the previous 22 years.
- Most had seen significant increases in attendance over the previous three years.
- 47% had seen over 10 professions of faith in Christ during the previous year, and 73% of those making professions remained active in the life of the church.
- Most had regularly scheduled events for members to share the gospel.

Positive Impact #2: Cross-cultural partnerships empower monocultural churches to thrive in a multicultural society.

In Chapter 3, Sonia stated that the multicultural church is one of the most important models for the future of American Christianity. But she was clear that it's not for everyone. There is and will continue to be a meaningful place for the monocultural church in any society.

First-generation immigrants prefer monocultural churches because of the language barrier. Latinos won't be attracted to Swahili-language churches. Even English-language first-generation churches I've attended, such as Liberian, Ghanaian, and Indian, are so culturally unique that most Christians from other backgrounds won't be attracted to them.

Most white Americans and African Americans prefer to worship with their own. Even if their churches are biblically sound, English-based, and warmly welcoming, there's still a significant cultural gap. If a pastor from a first-generation immigrant church, white American church, or African American church were to announce significant changes to the format of the service to attract those of other cultures, they will face strong opposition. Congregants of any monocultural background will reward their pastors for providing the style of worship they've always known and loved.

That's not a bad thing. When I eat sushi at a sushi restaurant, it's better than sushi at a restaurant that includes it among dozens of other items. There is a unique energy to worship and preaching in a roomful of Liberians (or other ethnicities) that will be lost if all churches become multicultural. I am an advocate of monocultural and multicultural churches working together in harmony, genuinely respecting each other's respective paradigms of ministry.

The biggest disadvantage of the monocultural church is that it typically only attracts people of its own culture. Thus, it cannot singlehandedly fulfill God's command to love all members of the Body of Christ. How do we resolve this tension? Here is the recommendation of the Lausanne Movement[3]:

All of us are agreed that in many situations a homogeneous unit church can be a legitimate and authentic church. Yet we are also agreed that it can never be complete in itself. Indeed, if it remains in isolation, it cannot reflect the universality and diversity of the Body of Christ. Nor can it grow into maturity. Therefore, every homogenous church must take active steps to broaden its fellowship in order to demonstrate visibly the unity and the variety of Christ's church. This will mean forging with other and different churches creative relationships which express the reality of Christian love, brotherhood, and interdependence.

Their point is that a monocultural church is able to answer Jesus' prayer in John 17:21 "That they may all be one," but cannot do it alone. It can only be accomplished through partnership with churches of other cultures.

Positive Impact #3: Cross-cultural church partnerships are the most likely path to raise up the next generation of ministry leaders with the qualities needed to create a vibrant future for American Christianity.

Positive Impact #2 primarily addresses the worship needs of the current generation of Christians. Positive Impact #3 addresses the markedly different worship needs of the upcoming generation.

In many Gen Z schools, there is no longer any majority group. Today's young people experience higher levels of diversity in their schools, workplaces, television, and social media than previous generations. They are more likely to befriend those of other cultures and to respond positively to multicultural worship than previous generations. Multicultural services may be more naturally attractive to them than monocultural ones.

Here's the bottom line: *Multicultural churches attract multicultural people.* Multicultural churches are more likely to succeed if they focus their attention on groups such as those of mixed race, those in mixed marriages, and second- and third-generation immigrants. These aren't only the best candidates for membership in multicultural churches; they're also the best candidates for leadership. Because second-generation immigrants are natively experienced in relating with both their parents' culture and American culture, they are ideal candidates to pastor multicultural churches.

Sadly, neither first-generation immigrant churches nor American churches are wired to empower the second generation. Most first-generation immigrant churches are small. They can only afford one pastor, and their cultures typically only empower older married men. Highly gifted 25- and 30-year-old second-generation immigrants rarely find empowerment for leadership in first-generation churches. And it would not dawn on most American churches to hire as their next pastor a second-generation Nigerian, Mexican, or Korean.

This means there is little job market for highly gifted second-generation ministry leaders. I believe that partnerships between American and immigrant churches will be more likely to create environments which will disciple second- and third-generation youth in English and empower them as young adults for ministry than churches working independently. The American church desperately needs their leadership!

Positive Impact #4: Churches engaged in healthy cross-cultural partnerships experience fresh momentum.

Later in this chapter I will share stories of Minnesota churches that have built wonderful cross-cultural partnerships. The kind of fresh momentum they experience is true at the denominational level as well as at the local church level.

The membership statistics of most American denominations over the past 30 years are not encouraging. Many have experienced declines of 40% or more. The denomination with the strongest retention rate I have seen is the Assemblies of God. Their 2022 statistics showed that 51% of their adherents are under the age of 35[4]. I've attended churches where hardly anyone is under 35! What's the reason for their high retention rate? Roughly 44% of the Assembly's adherents are multiethnic. They have invested heavily in making disciples and planting churches among our immigrant communities. While most American churches are in decline, immigrant churches have experienced comparatively strong growth rates. The Assembly's dedication to becoming a multiethnic body denomination-wide has resulted in numerical as well as spiritual growth.

I don't want to be guilty of false advertising. I'm not saying engaging in a cross-cultural partnership is guaranteed to generate numerical growth. It may or may not. But it is likely to generate Kingdom growth, bring a renewed sense of purpose, and bring joy in answering Jesus' prayer in John 17:21 "That they may all be one." And it might actually be fun!

3. Ordinary Churches are Successfully Doing It

Every good sermon closes with a moving story. I will close this lesson with several powerful stories. Over the past years, it's been my delight to worship in over 80 immigrant churches in the Twin Cities metro area. I've had the opportunity to dialogue with local American and immigrant pastors serving together in partnership. I believe these churches are on the cutting edge of the kind of change American churches need. While a few of these congregations are megachurches, most are small to medium, and all of them are making a significant Kingdom impact.

If you intend to teach this material yourself, I hope you will be able to identify stories from your own community or denomination. The more you expose people to others like themselves who have built successful cross-cultural partnerships, the more likely you will be able to persuade them they can succeed as well.

Bethel Christian Fellowship of St. Paul and the *All Nations Family of Churches.* In Chapter 4, I shared with you my experiences pastoring at the Beijing International Christian Fellowship. It is an example of the multi-congregational church, which I define as two or more congregations whose pastors regard themselves as a team of peers and engage in ministry together. There are two such examples in Minnesota, and All Nations Family of Churches is the older and larger of the two. Its story begins with Bethel Christian Fellowship of St. Paul.

Thirty years ago, Bethel was a primarily white church. As the demographics of its surrounding neighborhood began to change, church leadership chose to not relocate to the suburbs, but to remain and gradually become more multiethnic. As it did so, God brought to them not just individual families, but entire communities from specific ethnic groups. Their sponsorship of a Haitian refugee family led to other Haitian families joining their congregation as well. This led to the formation of their second congregation, the Haitian Christian Fellowship.

Today this fellowship of seven congregations is called the *All Nations Family of Churches,* two of which are English-language multicultural churches, and the remainder are ethnic churches worshipping in Nepali, Oromo, French, Creole, Karen Burmese, and Swahili. Each church has its own Board and financial systems, but share facilities, staff, and are all members of the Fellowship of Christian Assemblies. The pastors gather monthly for fellowship, learning, and prayer. They conduct quarterly joint worship events and engage in other shared ministries throughout the year.

La Casa del Padre and *Eden Prairie Assembly of God of Eden Prairie.* When Abdala Lopez planted Casa del Padre Church at a member's home in Eden Prairie, MN, she asked me to help her find a meeting facility. I introduced her to the leadership team of Eden Prairie Assembly of God. When the Assemblies church opened its facility to Casa del Padre, Pastor Abdala voluntarily changed their worship time from 5:00 PM to 11:00 AM, so their children and youth could receive English Bible education. When two Venezuelan members of the Assemblies church heard about La Casa del Padre, they volunteered to provide Spanish-language worship with a full band.

St. Michael's Lutheran and *Power of Gospel Churches of Bloomington.* Several years ago, the Oromo Ethiopian congregation Power of Gospel began to worship in the facility of a strong but graying white church, St. Michael's Lutheran of Bloomington. Observing that Power of Gospel had no systematic method of discipling its young people, the pastors of St. Michael's invited their high school youth to participate in their Wednesday evening confirmation classes. As the Ethiopian parents had opportunity to observe and trust these classes, over time the enrollment of Ethiopian youth outnumbered American youth. The two churches now combine their children's and youth ministries. As young people graduate from high school, they are given the opportunity to attend either the Oromo or English services, with the full blessing of both leadership teams.

Foundry College Church of Minneapolis, Twin Cities Hmong Baptist Church of Roseville and *Evangelical Formosan Church of the Twin Cities of St. Paul.* Not every cross-cultural church partnership in the Minneapolis area includes an American church.

Foundry College Church is an English-language, primarily East Asian church that was born out of campus ministry at the University of Minnesota. Its founders were second-generation East Asians who were mentored in disciple-making during their university years in Northern California. They began with a campus ministry that attracted both international students and second-plus-generation immigrants. Most of the leaders of Foundry College Church serve covocationally, giving them capacity to provide youth ministries to less-resourced churches. One such ministry at Foundry is *InterHigh*, which currently provides youth ministries to Twin Cities Hmong Baptist Church and Evangelical Formosan Church of the Twin Cities.

New Hope Church of New Hope. New Hope is one of several churches in the area using the "church within a church" model. When the leadership brought on a Latino pastor to launch a Spanish-language service, it did not create separate governance or financial systems for it. Instead, it launched a Spanish-language service in addition to its English-language service. The congregations share joint governance, budgeting, facilities, staff, and more. Children's and youth ministries in English are shared between the groups. When young people turn 19, they have the choice to worship at the Spanish or English services, with their parents' full blessing. This is one of the strongest models for serving both the first and second generations.

Resonate and *Vida Nueva Churches of Shakopee.* Within 10 months of launching their partnership in 2021, these two churches engaged in four levels of joint ministry: the sharing of space, midweek youth ministries, a summer outreach carnival, and a Thanksgiving food distribution outreach. That's the most rapid development of levels of partnership I've seen!

Gloria Dei Lutheran and *Royal Family Churches of Minneapolis.* When Gloria Dei opened its facility for Royal Family's worship, it was an aging white congregation that no longer had children's or youth ministries. Royal Family, by contrast, was an English-language, pan-African church full of young couples with children. During their first summer together, the two churches hosted a joint festival on the church grounds. American and African believers worked as teams to conduct the individual facets of the event. The following year, when Gloria Dei's pastor was transferred to another church, the elders asked Royal Family's Pastor Matthew Cephus to become their pastor as well. We have yet to see whether the two English-speaking congregations will merge into one, but either way they represent the power of healthy partnership.

Ethiopian Evangelical Church of St. Paul and *Perazim Church of Bloomington.* Pastor Endiryas Hawaz of St. Paul's Ethiopian Evangelical Church realized their ministries faced significant linguistic and cultural barriers in reaching their young people. Moved to meet the spiritual needs of their next generation, he hired a 1.5-generation Ethiopian pastor to form a youth group. In time, his son Ebenezer became the youth pastor. As the teenagers matured, the youth group evolved into a young adults' group. Over time the mother church commissioned this group to become Perazim Church, an English-language multiethnic church with deep Ethiopian roots. Now leading Perazim Church, Ebenezer realized he was one of only four second-generation Ethiopian pastors in the U.S. With few voices addressing their unique needs, he started a podcast named *Shaping the Culture.* This podcast now has hundreds of regular listeners from around the world.

The Multi-Congregational Church at Westwood Church's Bloomington campus. Westwood Community Church is a primarily white multi-site church with a passion to serve its immigrant community. When it developed its Bush Lake facility in Bloomington, it included a ministry center known as *The Hub*, with the purpose of resourcing, supporting, and providing work and worship space for immigrant church plants across the Twin Cities.

Today four churches of different races, denominations, and generations worship at Bush Lake and each church also has their own dedicated office space in The Hub. Pastor Ebenezer's Perazim Church is one of the four. Mauricio Dell pastors Destino Church, a 1.5-generation bilingual Spanish-English Latino congregation. Earnest Jeyaraja pastors Global Harvest, a first-generation Indian American church. The fourth congregation is Westwood's own primarily white congregation. Westwood is a Converge congregation, Destino is part of the Evangelical Covenant Church, Global Harvest is part of the Assemblies of God, and Perazim is independent. These four congregations have independent Boards and financial systems. While Westwood owns the facility, the four pastors work as a team to determine the ministry and facility use calendar. The pastors meet for lunch once a month for fellowship, with no church business allowed. They've found that relationship building is indispensable in building and maintaining a highly diverse team.

That is a sampling of the cross-cultural partnerships happening in the Minneapolis/St. Paul area. I regularly hear similar stories across North America as I coach cohorts of denominational leaders and pastors through *The Merging Streams Coalition*.

Coaching small group cohorts through The Merging Streams Coalition is the favorite part of my ministry as Executive Director of Immigrant Ministry Connections.

Each cohort brings together ministry leaders of different denominations, ethnicities and generations to discuss how we can most effectively motivate pastors and everyday Christians to desire healthy cross-cultural partnerships. The content of Chapters 6-8 of this book serves as our core curriculum, and our discussions focus on implementing the principles of those chapters. You can learn more about The Merging Streams Coalition at our website, www.immigrantministry.com/mergingstreams.

I hope this chapter enables you to build a compelling case for cross-cultural church partnerships that will multiply the number of believers willing to serve alongside you. In the next chapter, we move beyond **why** to discuss the **who** question of launching healthy partnerships. Not everyone in your church will desire to engage in a cross-cultural ministry, but you can form a small team that will accomplish significant ministry and grow over time.

7

Quick Start Guideline 2: Build a Small but Healthy Team

I n Chapter 6, we addressed *why* American and immigrant Christians should desire engagement in joint ministry. Here, we will discuss *who*, describing the team you need to launch a healthy partnership. Three elements are involved:

1. Commit to a relational orientation over a task orientation.
2. Identify your Three Indispensable Persons.
3. Mobilize a small but healthy team from your congregation.

I realize that many visionaries want everyone in the church to buy into the vision, but that's not realistic. In any church, a handful of people will always be opposed to cross-cultural partnership, and a greater number will be simply disinterested. You can launch a healthy partnership with a small team. As you share your initial victories with the congregation, more people will develop passion for the ministry.

1. Commit to a Relational Orientation Over a Task Orientation

Most global cultures are far more relational than America's highly individualistic culture. We Americans are not likely to be aware of this, since we typically socialize with those as individualistic as ourselves. This leads us to regard our behavior as a universal norm others should follow. But most don't.

Pastors from African and Latino cultures have shared with me that American pastors and churches come short of their expectations of hospitality. I've seen church partnerships where the gears of ministry turn smoothly, but there is dissatisfaction due to relational distance. These pastors see themselves as cogs in an efficient and effective but impersonal American ministry machine. They will typically not raise any objections, because their American partners have been so generous to them. But the dissatisfaction lingers.

We type-A, businesslike Americans tend to view our relationships—both with people and God—from a functional perspective. It's easy to focus exclusively on the facets of salvation that are an instantaneous transaction, including the forgiveness of sins and the imputation of righteousness. But we may neglect the relational side of salvation. Jesus said in Revelation 3:20, "Behold, I stand at the door and knock. If anyone hears my voice and opens the door, I will come in to him and eat with him, and he with me." Jesus is not looking for a transaction, but a relationship. He isn't envisioning fast food or a drive-through. He's desiring a seven-course meal where we sit together and share our lives.

That's the kind of relationship immigrant Christians are seeking from their American friends. As my Argentine pastor friend Mauricio Dell says, "If the only time you and I meet is when there are problems, then our relationship will be entirely about problems."

Most American and immigrant churches who share space are nothing more than "religious roommates." That's not genuine partnership. I've seen other partnerships that share ministries such as children's, youth, worship, and community service, yet remain politely distant. It's when pastors move beyond theology and programming into relationship that genuine partnership is formed.

We American pastors love Big Hairy Audacious Goals. We are very adept at crafting meticulously worded strategic visions, doctrinal statements, and building use covenants. But we may not realize how counterproductive it is to craft these documents without input from our partners. One morning I had coffee with an American pastor who had emailed detailed documents to a prospective immigrant partner for completion. He asked me, "What was that pastor's name, again?" The two pastors never met, had no personal connection, and yet the American pastor was requiring detailed documentation!

This is not how relationships are formed in most global cultures. Strategic plans, denominational distinctives, and facilities are important. But none of them are made in the image of God, and none will last into eternity. Only human beings will. May I suggest that the first step of your potential partnership is not to discuss strategic alignment, but to share a meal together?

The fault is not wholly on the American side. I've met numerous immigrant pastors who are quite relational with their own people but have no desire for partnership with

Americans. When an immigrant pastor in the Minneapolis area contacts me, it's almost always because they're looking for a place to meet. Many have no desire for partnership with a host church. They see the relationship as nothing more than that of a landlord and tenant.

For those of you who skim books, take note. Below is possibly the most important sentence in this entire book: **The line in the sand between success and failure in forming a healthy cross-cultural church partnership is the determination of an American pastor and an immigrant pastor to embark on a relational and ministry journey together.**

In Chapter 8, I will demonstrate that your partnership need not be too draining on your time programmatically. But it will demand your time relationally. I realize most pastors are already overworked, and do not cherish the thought of adding another responsibility. I'm asking you to add a new significant relationship. We all know that America's future will be multicultural than its past. This impacts the way we do ministry. *Any church that is not effective at some level of cross-cultural ministry will become irrelevant to American society.*

2. Identify Your Three Indispensable Persons

There are three key people without whose engagement a cross-cultural church partnership will stagnate:

- The senior pastor of the American church
- The Connector of the American church
- The senior pastor of the immigrant church

I am not listing the Connector of the immigrant church, because in most cases the senior pastor of the immigrant church also serves as its Connector. No matter how many gifted individuals engage in cross-cultural ministry in your church, the partnership will not flourish until these three people build meaningful relationships with one another.

Let's talk first about the senior pastor of the American church. There are certain qualities he must possess for the partnership to thrive.

- He must fully embrace the vision of the cross-cultural partnership. Such partnerships are particularly vulnerable during transitions of the senior pastor of either the American or the immigrant church. I've observed partnerships where the previous American pastor had developed a close relationship with the immigrant pastor, but his successor did not share the same passion. In such cases, the partnership typically languishes.
- He must be the primary vision caster. The Connector and other members can participate in casting the vision, but without heartfelt endorsement from the senior pastor, the partnership will not gain momentum.
- He needs to have good chemistry with the senior pastor of the immigrant church. If someone else serves as the Connector, the two senior pastors need not maintain frequent communication, but they must like, respect, and trust each other.
- The senior American pastor may or may not have strong cross-cultural skills. I've seen both kinds build healthy partnerships. If the lead pastor is aware that he does not have strong cross-cultural skills, his best

course of action is to appoint someone else to serve as their church's Connector.

- Most immigrant pastors desire partnership with American pastors who are theologically and morally conservative. The vast majority of immigrant Christians are more conservative than their American counterparts. When I speak with immigrant pastors in the Twin Cities who are looking for space in an American church, their number one request is to not be partnered with a church that endorses the progressive sexual agenda. A number have said explicitly that they do not want to meet in a church building displaying a rainbow flag.

- He may or may not be the Connector for the partnership. For the senior pastor to serve as the Connector, he must have adequate time to dedicate to the role. If someone else holds the position of Connector, this does not prevent the senior pastor or others from speaking with the immigrant pastor at any time. The Connector does not exist to control the relationship, but to ensure its relational depth.

Now let's discuss the Connector. This is the liaison or lead point person who manages the relationship. The qualifications here are true for both the Connectors of the American and the immigrant churches. In most cases, the lead pastor of the immigrant church is also their Connector.

- The Connector must be *delighted* with the opportunity to build a friendship with someone from another culture. If the Connector is simply assigned the task, the relationship will not flourish. The relationship between the two Connectors cannot only be about ministry programming and theology. It must be about life and family. The two Connectors must take the lead in helping their congregations desire cross-cultural friendships.

- The Connectors must agree to meet at least monthly. More often is even better. Those meetings should be face-to-face, over a meal or tea whenever possible. Of course, the Connectors will need to discuss church business, but I recommend that at least half of their time together be given to relationship building.

- When they begin, the Connectors may not have highly developed cross-cultural skills. What they need is love. Specifically, they must develop skills of listening and asking good questions. I recommend that Connectors consider using the questions in the Implementation Study Guide to direct their conversations.

- The Connector of the American church needs to be a trusted insider who has the ear of the senior pastor. The senior pastor must be delighted that this individual holds the role of Connector and trusts their opinions and views. This gives the Connector opportunity to share feedback from the immigrant pastor that the American church leadership might otherwise not receive.

- Many American churches have complex systems, policies and point persons regarding facility usage, budgets, children's ministries, and more. Most immigrant pastors hold full-time job outside the church and lack time to understand the American church's complex systems. The Connector can serve as a gateway between the immigrant pastor and the American church's systems, engaging with the appropriate parties on the immigrant church's behalf.

Now let's talk about qualities the senior pastor of the immigrant church must have.

- He must be theologically orthodox. Approximately 20% of the immigrant churches I've attended demonstrate extreme levels of Prosperity Theology or other cultish teaching. Few evangelical congregations would desire partnership with them.
- He must have general but not necessarily identical theological agreement with the American church. The American church must determine whether they will require partners to become members of their denomination. I hope this will be rare. There are approximately 100 million Christians in China, and none of them are members of American denominations. Expecting global Christians to cherish the distinctives of Western denominations isn't very realistic. Americans may not realize that 80% of Christians who come from non-Western countries hold to some level of Pentecostal belief and practice. It is wise for American church leaders to become comfortable around the expression of supernatural gifts, so that they can help their congregations be equally relaxed in the presence of such manifestations.
- He should have a strong desire to build relationships with pastors of other ethnicities.
- He should be open to discipling their children in English, and to empowering them for leadership as young adults. It is best to tread softly and slowly here. Many first-generation immigrants want their children to love the language and culture of their

homelands as much as they do. We should affirm this desire. But it must be coupled with the understanding that their children and grandchildren will be English-dominant and think like Americans. Be patient, listen, love, and gently point them in the direction of discipling their children in English. This is an area of ministry where you can provide of invaluable assistance to them.

- The two pastors and leadership teams must identify *a shared spiritual passion*. The best way to do this is to *attend each other's worship services*. This is where you have the opportunity to experience "the real deal." I've met immigrant pastors who were quite pleasant at the dinner table. But when they're on the platform in their own churches, a few of them become authoritarian, manipulative, and sensationalistic. When the leadership teams of both churches enjoy each other's preaching, worship, and prayer, you have the basis for a strong partnership.

- Once you have this passion, be sure to *regularly pray together*. I've not said much about prayer in this book. The spiritual dynamics of forming cross-cultural partnerships are critical, but they mostly overlap with the spiritual dynamics of launching other new ministries. The disciplines your team has developed in intercession and listening to God in other settings will serve them well in this process. Beyond doubt, each individual engaged in the discussion should engage in personal prayer. But God has given equal authority in prayer to people of all nations. Engaging in joint prayer reinforces the shared spiritual passion you are cultivating. It helps us to humbly discover that global Christians pray powerfully in many different ways. And their prayers bring answers from heaven!

3. Mobilize a Small but Healthy Team from your Congregation

Now that we've talked about the three people who are indispensable to your partnership, let's talk more broadly. First, I will share ideas relevant to your Board and staff, then to the entire congregation.

Bring your Board and staff into alignment with the vision. Before raising the idea of partnership with your entire Board or staff, it's wise to anticipate important one-on-one conversations in advance. If you know some members who are likely to strongly advocate for the partnership, their influence will strengthen your appeal to the larger group.

It's also wise to anticipate those Board or staff members who may not share your desire for cross-cultural partnership. Meeting with them individually before bringing the suggestion to the group will allow them space to raise their concerns without bringing unnecessary tension to the group meeting.

It isn't necessary for all your Board and staff members to be equally passionate about your partnership. You need a few to be deeply passionate, most to be generally supportive, and some to be curiously watchful. If you follow the three guidelines outlined in Chapters 6-8, you will experience small but growing wins that will move your leadership team over time to be increasingly supportive of the vision for partnership.

Bring the vision before the entire congregation. Once you've won general support from your Board and staff, it's time to create passion for the partnership among the congregation.

In many ways, you can approach members of your congregation as you do your Board and staff. It's always helpful to gain the support of those who will be passionate to engage in the new partnership. You can gain early wins by meeting individually with those you already know to be passionate about cross-cultural ministry.

By the time you announce this vision from the platform, the Three Indispensable People should have a healthy working relationship, the Board and staff should be in alignment, and the key drivers of the new initiative should be identified. Now it's time to use the pulpit, announcements, website, social media, education, small groups, and other communications platforms to generate support and engagement for the partnership.

As noted, it's unrealistic to expect your entire congregation to be onboard with this vision (or any other vision). As with any new initiative, there will always be the visionaries, early adopters, early majority, late majority, and laggards. I suggest you begin with an initiative that will bring little change to your church as a whole, especially to your worship service. It will help if you can assure the congregation about facets of the church that will remain unchanged as you launch your new partnership.

That is the core of ***who*** is necessary to build a healthy cross-cultural partnership. Now let's look at the more tactile issues of ***what*** and ***how*** to conduct a successful small-scale initial launch event for your new partnership.

8

Quick Start Guideline #3: Conduct a Simple, Small-Scale, Joint Launch Event

Now we come to the third and final step in our Quick Start Guide, which is to conduct a simple, small-scale, joint launch event. This is the *what* and *how* aspect of forming your partnership. You've already done the hard work of casting a vision for *why* the partnership is necessary. Then you've identified *who* are the right people to engage with you. These two steps are much harder than the more straightforward work of planning and conducting a one-time event.

You will experience a higher likelihood of disappointment if your initial joint ministry event is complex, expensive, and long-term. You're more likely to succeed if you begin with a small-scale, short-term, inexpensive project. I recommend beginning with a one-time event like a potluck, carnival, concert, or evangelistic outreach. This will enable you to gain small wins and gradually increase the level of acceptance and ownership among your congregation.

Envision this event as *two churches jointly serving the community*, not as *one church serving another*. If you envision this event as an American church serving an immigrant church, it reinforces the concept that the American church is superior because of its greater wealth, education, and organizational capacity. Such a relationship is top-down, failing to recognize the giftedness and value of both churches' contributions.

It is important to *engage the leadership teams of both churches from the very first meeting.* Conducting even one planning meeting without including your immigrant partner communicates clearly that their input is peripheral. Both churches must be involved at every step in the process. Let me list areas where both churches must be involved.

- *Choosing the event*: If the American church simply opens its existing ministry programming to its partnering immigrant church, they will not take the same level of ownership as if the event was their idea. It's like being invited to someone else's home. Your host may be cordial, but you are still aware that their home is not your home. You would never help yourself to the refrigerator, hang your pictures on the wall, or rearrange the furniture. When both churches are engaged from the beginning in the planning and execution of the event, there is a higher likelihood that the event will provide value to everyone.

- *Planning the event:* Both churches must be engaged in determining the date, time, location, price, and people who will be engaged. This does not mean that both churches must be equally involved in performing the work. One congregation may be substantially larger than the other, providing more of the workers. What matters is that both churches have an important voice in planning the details. If the American church staff are full-time in ministry and the immigrant partners have full-time jobs outside the church, meetings should be conducted on evenings or weekends so that both sides can be involved.

- *Funding the event:* It's best to assess the relative size and incomes of both congregations to set a realistic expectation of how much of the cost they should bear. Each church should bear some financial responsibility.

- *Conducting the event:* Members of both churches should participate in each facet of the event. If you hold a carnival, it would be unwise to have the Americans grilling the meat while the immigrants conduct the children's activities. Americans and immigrants should be grilling the meat and running the children's games together. One goal of the event is to build as many relationships as possible. If there is a language barrier, divide your translators as necessary so many people can serve together.

- *Celebrating the event:* One indispensable ingredient in your joint activity is *fun*. Celebrate together! We all build relationships more naturally when we're laughing. Events are more fun when you include food, music, and children. If you are conducting a more serious event like food distribution, be sure to hold a joint debrief event afterward so both churches can celebrate.

- *Evaluating the event*: Both sides should be involved in evaluating the event. What went well? What did not go so well? What could be done differently next time? Joint evaluation will help both sides determine how relationships are progressing and whether you wish to repeat that particular event in the future.

There are three kinds of people the American church should involve to receive the maximum benefit from this joint ministry event.

- *Your active members.* Not everyone in your church will be interested in engaging in this activity, but many will. You only need the engagement of a few people to conduct a successful small-scale event.
- *Your lapsed members.* You may want to engage those who have not returned to your church after COVID. Some may be hesitant to return to a larger crowd but might be open to an event with a smaller crowd, or an event conducted outdoors. This may be a good avenue of opportunity for them to begin to reengage with your church.
- *Your youth.* As I've said before, today's young people are growing up in a much more multicultural society than previous generations. They are more innately able to work together with people of other cultures. Many American churches desire to see some of their young people serve as cross-cultural missionaries. But while it is vital for the church to share the gospel globally, it is equally imperative to bring the gospel to all peoples locally. The majority of your young people will never live overseas. But they can become Christ-loving, multicultural people who naturally share their faith with all peoples in their communities.

Popular launch events

There are many kinds of one-time activities that make ideal launch events for cross-cultural church partnerships. Some possibilities include food distribution, youth rallies, joint worship services, picnics, baptisms, and carnivals.

One popular option is to celebrate an ethnic festival like Cinco de Mayo, Diwali, or Chinese New Year. When Sherry and I lived in Beijing, Chinese New Year was the biggest event of the year. It was a 10-day holiday. On New Year's Eve, everyone set off fireworks. Nobody could get to sleep until two o'clock in the morning! Every family made delicious homemade dumplings. If you invite Chinese friends to your church for Chinese New Year, they will love you if all you do is purchase frozen dumplings at the local Asian market. Better yet, ask them to make the dumplings! The very fact that you were interested in their culture will go a long way toward building relational bonds.

As I said at the beginning of this chapter, addressing the questions of **what** and **how** is simpler than addressing the questions of **why** and **who**. Conducting a simple one-time initial launch event is a relatively straightforward matter of planning details.

Increasing the scale of your joint ministries can be equally straightforward. If you started with a one-time event, consider making it an ongoing quarterly or annual event. Events focused around Easter, Christmas, or your partner's national holidays naturally lend themselves to becoming annually recurring events. Some churches collaborate for summertime carnivals or Thanksgiving food distribution. Some hold quarterly joint worship services. There are many examples of recurring seasonal events that build strong relationships between churches.

It's important to celebrate your successful ministries from the platform, social media, and other communications outlets. Creating visibility for the successes of your partnership will help to generate support and engagement from your congregation.

It's quite common for cross-cultural church partnerships to begin with a discussion of sharing facilities. Many partnerships begin with the sharing of facilities, and later develop joint relationships and ministries. Differing cultural expectations can lead to tension over facility usage. More partnerships break down over the smell of curry in the kitchen than over theological divisions. There are different cultural expectations on a number of issues such as unattended children, equipment usage, cleanliness, legal liability, and more. Both sides must clearly communicate in advance about these issues.

Because many of our practices regarding facility usage are subconscious and unwritten, I recommend that any two churches considering sharing a facility begin by drafting a joint (and if necessary, bilingual) Church Facility Stewardship Covenant. This is similar to premarital counseling. The more issues a couple discuss before they marry, the less surprises they will experience. You will find a template for a Church Facility Stewardship Covenant at the end of this book.

Once two churches have determined that they will continue to work together in a long-term partnership, whether or not that partnership includes sharing facilities, it's wise to hold some form of partnership inauguration service. This can entail leadership teams visiting each other's services, or both churches holding a joint celebration service. The service should include the inauguration of the partnership, recognition of the leadership teams, celebration of joint ministries you've already shared, and prayer for one another. If the partnership includes use of a facility, additional touches can include public signing of a Church Facility

Stewardship Covenant and the bestowal of keys. Other positive elements to such a celebration service include joint participation in worship, preaching and communion, and the sharing of a joint meal afterwards.

Most problems that arise in cross-cultural church partnerships are relational, specifically involving lack of communication between the Three Indispensable Persons. In the next chapter, we will resume Susan's story as she walks pastors through the process of keeping partnerships healthy for the long term.

9

Keeping Your Partnership
Healthy for the Long Term

Within months of the release of Susan's *Quick Start Guide*, Sonia had distributed it to churches in several districts. It piqued the curiosity of many pastors, who'd never seen anything in print on this subject before. An understanding of the Three Indispensable Persons led to discussions at staff and Board levels, a key indicator of success.

Sonia and Susan had more frequent conversations about situations they were facing. On this call, Sonia spoke with Susan from an available meeting room at DataConnect's Warsaw office.

"The elders of Lake Erie Parkerite Church are struggling to obtain decisions from the elders of their partnering Latino congregation," said Sonia. "Their constitution and bylaws require decisions by a partnering organization be passed by a two-thirds majority. Ríos de Agua Viva Church doesn't even have a constitution or bylaws. Pastor Jorge just talks to the members of the congregation until he identifies a direction they accept. Nobody votes on anything. It's how they've always done it. This greatly frustrates the Lake Erie Board, which requires formally ratified decisions signed by a Secretary. The Chairman of their Board, an attorney, offered to help Ríos de Agua Viva draw up a constitution, but they don't see the point. They just see a constitution as another requirement to fit within an Anglo system."

"The whole concept of governance is so cultural," said Susan. "If the Jerusalem Church required formally ratified Board decisions from the Philippian Church, I wonder what they would have received."

Sonia nodded. "Yes, it's like putting Saul's armor on David. DataConnect could never survive legally without carefully written policies. There's nothing wrong with churches having detailed governance documents as well. We just need to accept that it isn't required by the Bible. And that means churches with complex governance systems need to find ways to relate to churches with simple, informal governance systems."

"Communication styles are just as diverse," Susan added. "I love seeing Pastors Jeremy and Rashed working together, but they struggle to communicate effectively. Pastor Jeremy writes brilliantly crafted, detailed emails. But Pastor Rashed grew up in a refugee camp. Nobody in the camp wrote emails, used a calendar app, or posted selfies. They just survived day by day.

At first, I asked Pastor Jeremy to cc me on emails to Rashed, so I could simply notify him to check his inbox. But he usually didn't reply to all the items on Jeremy's list, and that was frustrating. I finally realized that Rashed isn't an 'email guy' but a 'text guy.' He promptly replies to text messages. So I realized part of my job as their Connector is to 'translate' email to text. Rashed speaks fine English, so language isn't a barrier. Email is the barrier. Now when I get a complex email from Jeremy, I text the questions to Rashed one-by-one and call him if necessary. Then I take his responses and write an email reply to Jeremy. Email-to-text translation is a lot easier than language translation, and it gets the job done."

"The use of technology is certainly different across cultures," Sonia said. "Members of the Ugandan congregation partnering with Pittsburgh Parkerite won't use their church's app to volunteer for service events. But when Sister Jesca texts volunteers to ask for help, they will reliably come. But they might not show up at 2:00 sharp!" she quickly added. Then she leaned in. "Is there a common issue you see more often than any other?"

"There is," Susan said. "It's communication issues. Sometimes it's miscommunication, but more typically it's a lack of communication at all.

The more pastors I talk to, the more I realize that consistent, open communication is missing in most partnerships. And that weakens every other aspect of the partnership. It's just like a marriage. A couple that communicates well can work through nearly any issue. But a couple that fails to communicate can stumble over minor issues.

When I wrote the *Quick Start Guide*, I made it clear in Guideline #2 that partnerships will stumble if the lead American pastor, lead immigrant pastor, and American Connector don't have regular, quality communications. When pastors began to contact me about tensions within their partnerships, at first, I focused on the immediate concerns they raised. Now I begin by asking about the Three Indispensable Persons. If those three people haven't communicated in a while, there needs to be relationship building before the immediate problem can be addressed in a healthy manner.

My husband Bill says that half of computer problems can be fixed by just restarting the computer, and he won't help anyone troubleshoot an issue until they restart their computer at least once. I'm at the point now where I get the Connectors talking before I'll address major issues with them."

"Sometimes I wish I could reboot my admin," Sonia said, laughing. "It sounds like pastors default to task orientation instead of relationship orientation. No matter how well they understand their need to change, the transition is slow and full of setbacks."

"Yes," said Susan. "My friends in real estate tell me that the top three factors determining the value of a property are location, location, and location. I guess the top three factors in ensuring the health of a cross-cultural partnership are communication, communication, and communication.

Ever since the *Quick Start Guide* got out, pastors are asking me about advanced lessons. Right now, my response is that the advanced step is to never stop repeating the first steps.

I've really come to the place of believing that *maintaining the health of a cross-cultural partnership over the long haul comes down to two things: never stop listening, and never stop learning.*"

Susan rolled out the tension in her shoulders. "I can't stop listening in this job! I keep meeting people from new cultures and from different generations within those cultures. And even with the ones I think I know best, like Pastor Alfonso, I still wind up experiencing lots of surprises. When I only dealt with people who look like me, everything was more predictable and routine. Now sometimes I have no idea what's going on!

I'm not complaining. I really love all these new brothers and sisters. I'm just learning that complexity and confusion is my new normal."

"It's been my new normal since I took the HR position at DataConnect," Sonia said. "And it's America's new normal as well. All of us need to realize that our society is made up of people with different perspectives, and that affects how they communicate and build relationships.

I appreciate it when you said, 'never stop listening.' There are times we can learn through conversations with others. But not always. A Parkerite church in Portland is working with a Karen Burmese congregation. They came through refugee camps and had low levels of literacy. The leaders of the church held the best conversations they could through translators, but it was pretty rough. Then they discovered a second-generation bilingual Karen attending university in Chicago. She understood Karen and American cultures very well. Because she is well-educated and articulate, she could explain Karen culture in ways the newly arrived Karen could not.

Nobody is capable of understanding the myriad of cultures in the U.S. It would be horribly unfair of me to expect an American pastor to have deep understanding of Indian culture—and five other cultures he's partnering with. I certainly don't have high levels of competence with the seventeen countries I engage at DataConnect. My goal in HR is not cultural *competence* but cultural *sensitivity*. Americans who haven't lived in the homeland of their guest congregation will never become experts in their culture. And most of us first-generation immigrants will not develop the same expertise in American culture as you native-born. Neither side should aim for native-level understanding of each other's culture. But both sides should aim for cultural sensitivity."

"That's a reasonable goal," said Susan. "I appreciate that you have invited me to enroll in the Master's in Cross-Cultural Ministry at Parker Seminary. But I really want to find solutions that work for busy pastors and everyday Christians. It makes sense that professional missionaries spend years learning linguistics, sociology, and anthropology. I'm sure we can glean from their insights. But those insights need to be boiled down to the level of everyday people who don't use insider jargon.

There are certain things we expect every American to learn, like nutrition, money management, and traffic regulations. You don't get a degree to do those things; they're just part of everyday life. I'm coming to the conviction that relating to different cultures and generations isn't something reserved for the experts, but for everyone in the U.S. And it shouldn't require formal schooling; it's just part of our worlds that we all have to figure out as we go through daily life."

"There will always be the tension between formal and informal education," said Sonia. "Each has its unique advantages and disadvantages, and we need both."

"Agreed," said Susan. "Well, I need to run. I'm off for our monthly pastors' luncheon at Samurai Sushi. I'm really proud of the four pastors working in partnership with Fragrant Hills. They've really bonded over the past months. And it's interesting to see how these partnerships have affected Fragrant Hills. We've certainly become more culturally sensitive, but we're still mostly white. I think we're settling into more of a multi-congregational church model than a multicultural church model."

"I can't wait to hear more about it," said Sonia. "I admire your courage in trying sushi. Somehow, I cannot wrap my Indian mind around eating raw fish and seaweed. I'll stick with lamb curry and naan any day. Greet the Columbus pastors for me."

10

Multicultural Church or Multi-Congregational Church?

S usan arrived early at Samurai Sushi to reserve a table for the Columbus Fellowship of Global Churches. That was the name chosen by the pastors working as a team in partnership with Fragrant Hills Church. Sometimes they just called it "the Columbus Fellowship" or used its acronym CFGC.

Susan was grateful that the entire Columbus Fellowship had been holding monthly lunch meetings since April. As the Connector for Fragrant Hills, she had built relations with each pastor. But real value came from all the pastors of the Fellowship building relationships with one another. To encourage this, she conducted as much business as she could during their one-on-one conversations, freeing more of their monthly luncheon time for relationship building.

Work schedules made a Saturday luncheon their only option. The group alternated between restaurants of different cuisines, not always from their homelands.

"Last year I probably would have thought sushi was Vietnamese food," said Pastor Jeremy. "Now I realize that it's part of Japanese cuisine."

"People mix Asians up all the time," said Pastor Nguyen. "Lots of Americans see us Asians and say, 'You guys are all Chinese.'"

Pastor Victoria grinned. "And when they see us Latinos they say, 'You guys are all Mexicans.'"

Pastor Rashed also added, "And when they see high school students from anywhere in Africa, they say 'You're just another black kid.'"

"We all have misconceptions about one another," said Susan. "Hopefully these lunch gatherings help all of us address these issues with our congregations."

After asking their server about various types of sushi, sashimi, tempura, and noodles, Susan shared the only piece of news relevant to all of them, an update about the launch of The Columbus Welcome Center. Now only three months old, the Welcome Center provided immigration legal assessment and services. Two members of Fragrant Hills took the 40 hours of online training from the Department of Justice necessary to provide immigrant legal services. The Columbus Fellowship hoped that the Columbus Welcome Center would grow to include ESL services, driver's education, after-school tutoring, and more.

With her report completed, each pastor shared about their personal lives.

Pastor Jeremy spoke first. Susan noticed he had become much more relaxed and open during lunch meetings with his fellow pastors. He remained his type-A efficient self when conducting church business, but understood the necessity of entering an unhurried and relational state when they were together. She also knew that certain elders of Fragrant Hill did not regard these global pastors to be as highly gifted and skilled as their American counterparts. Pastor Jeremy had prioritized relating with them as a peer, allowing him to effectively communicate his high esteem for their giftedness with his leadership team.

"I want to thank all of you for the love you poured out on Connie after her third miscarriage. We've been struggling with infertility for years, and really hoped this third time God would give us a healthy baby. But that wasn't his plan for us. It isn't easy coming to church wearing a smile while so many other families our age already have children. Connie was so blessed by the ladies who stopped by our home during her recovery period. Their fellowship and prayers meant so much to her. And it's been helpful for me to speak with each of you about this struggle."

Pastor Rashed spoke next. "My heart is so burdened for my brother and sister who still live in refugee camps in Kenya and Uganda. They walked hundreds of miles to escape the ongoing violence in South Sudan. My wife and I are blessed that we received our visas to come to the United States. Everyone in our congregation has heartbreaking stories of the hardships they endured during the civil war or while growing up in overcrowded refugee camps. Every one of them has close relatives who long to join them in America. Some of them have received words from the Lord that their loved ones will be joining them. But the wait is so long. There is nothing we can do except wait upon the Lord and the government."

"We've come to love your people so deeply," said Pastor Nguyen. "Most of the time the news only tells us about wars in a few countries, like Ukraine, Afghanistan, and Israel. But we rarely hear about countries across the world that are plagued with chronic unrest, leaving refugees fleeing to nearby countries. We love your people and pray they will soon be reunited with their loved ones."

The group spent a few minutes in prayer for the families of Pastor Rashed's congregation before moving on to Pastors Alfonso and Victoria.

"I'm so grateful for the good jobs our sons have taken," said Pastor Alfonso. "Both of them received technical training at Cox Technical Institute. Enrique has become a machinist and Hector an elevator mechanic. These are very good jobs for our young people. You know, Pastor Nguyen, our young people aren't headed off for Harvard like yours are." Everyone laughed. "But many aren't finishing high school at all. I'm grateful for the programs that help them find careers with good salaries that will support a family.

And we're also grateful for the way members of Fragrant Hills have come alongside our people and helped them figure out how things work here. The Columbus Welcome Center has been so helpful to us and to Pastor Rashed's congregation in processing their immigration papers. All this paperwork is so complicated and expensive! It's a great blessing to have brothers and sisters serve us in this way."

"And to do it through our churches," added Pastor Victoria. "People know that La Luz del Mundo and Fragrant Hills are churches that want to help people move forward in the process of completing their papers.

One of my greatest struggles is feeling accepted as a Christian leader. In my homeland women are recognized as pastors. Pastor Alfonso and I graduated from Bible school together, and were ordained at the same time as well. I respect that we Parkerites hold a belief called 'complementarianism.' It still feels like an odd compromise that because I'm ordained by a Guatemalan denomination in my homeland I'm recognized as 'a pastor' but not 'one of *our* pastors.' I appreciate that Pastor Jeremy has been an advocate for me in the Great Lakes district."

Pastor Nguyen was the last of the pastors to speak. "I am burdened for my grandchildren. Even though they are ethnically Vietnamese, their thinking is the same as to all their other Gen Z classmates. At such early ages they are exposed to pornography, gender politics, social media, and so much more. I have no idea how to relate with them.

When my own children were young, we insisted that they learn to worship in Vietnamese fashion. We wanted them to love our language and culture as deeply as we did. We taught them Bible stories from the Vietnamese Bible and sung from the Vietnamese hymnbook. But we failed to realize that their heart language was English. It took us by surprise when they dropped out of church after graduation from high school. Now their children have very little Christian exposure. Today we would be grateful if our children and grandchildren received Christian input from anyone. But we were twenty years too late realizing this.

As you know, our congregation is aging. It is difficult for me to provide direction for our elders. Many still want to worship according to the traditions of home. Others know if we continue down this path, within twenty years we will have to close down the church. I'm grateful that we've all agreed that our remaining children will participate in Fragrant Hills' children's and youth ministries. This has been quite well received. Pastors Alfonso and Victoria, I hope your people will realize these things while there is still time."

"Yes," said Pastor Alfonso. "Our people are very protective of their children. They gave up so much when they came to the U.S., not just possessions, but also respect and honor. Many have pinned all their hopes for the future on their children. Some of them see the American church as 'liberal' because they allow things like tattoos, earrings, makeup, green hair, and shorts. We have a saying, 'The devil speaks English.' We keep working to change this thinking, but it will take time for some of them to come around."

"What about you, Susan?" asked Pastor Rashed. "What's been happening in your life?"

"I've been spending more time with Mom since Dad passed away suddenly," Susan replied. "It's been a difficult transition for her. She keeps busy connecting with friends and serving at her church. The hardest time is after she returns home. It's just so quiet around the house. It's really hard for her to handle the loneliness. Now that our kids have all grown and gone, Bill and I are discussing if it might work for Mom to live with us. But her entire social network is in Cincinnati, and she's well cared for there.

I want to show you a picture of something my mom has been working on." Susan showed her cell phone to the group. "Mom has taken up quilting since Dad passed, and this is what she's working on right now."

"Such beautiful colors!" said Pastor Victoria. "Does your mom have a particular idea in mind when she picks out the fabric and pattern?"

"Over the past months, as I've shared your stories with her, she's come to appreciate the beauty and diversity of our churches, Susan replied. "She's named this one 'The Columbus Fellowship of Global Churches Quilt' in honor of you. Its pattern and colors were chosen to represent who we are as a Fellowship."

"How so?" asked Pastor Jeremy.

Susan pointed at different spots in the picture. "Different aspects of the quilt represent the three models of our churches: the monocultural church, the multicultural church, and the multi-congregational church.

Let's start with the solid blue star in the middle of the quilt. It's made out of one piece of fabric and has only one color. It represents monocultural churches like Pastor Nguyen's Hoi Thanh Church. Because their worship is conducted in the Vietnamese language, it appeals only to people who speak that language. That's not bad. I love worshipping with Hoi Thanh. I simply accept that it's monocultural.

Now look at the bright floral diamonds surrounding the star. They're each made from one piece of fabric with a multicolored floral design. It represents multicultural churches like La Luz del Mundo. Pastors Alfonso and Victoria have brothers and sisters from many different countries—Mexico, Peru, Venezuela, Uruguay, Ecuador, and more. And some Anglos, too. But they're all together in one Spanish-language service.

But when you step back and look at the quilt as a whole, what you see represents the multi-congregational church. I define the multi-congregational church as *three or more congregations whose pastors regard themselves as peers and engage in joint ministry.* The complete quilt represents the beauty of the four churches that make up the Columbus Fellowship of Global Churches. Some parts have only one color, other parts have two or more, but the overall quilt is beautifully multicolored."

"That's a great analogy," said Pastor Jeremy. "Is there any chance we can purchase that quilt from your mom?"

"She intends to donate it to the church when she comes for the anniversary of the launching of the Columbus Fellowship," Susan replied.

"That's something to really look forward to," said Pastor Nguyen.

"Yes, and I have something else for you to look forward to," Susan replied. "You really understand the issue of losing the second generation. It's true of immigrant churches of all ethnicities. Most conversations about cross-cultural partnerships focus on cultural differences. But we're realizing that generational differences are just as acute. So Parker Seminary is hosting a conference next spring titled 'The All Generations Summit.' They've asked Sonia to invite workshop presenters. I'm assisting her in that process. I'll be sure and let you know as we have specific details."

"Be sure to add me to that email list," said Pastor Jeremy. The other pastors asked to be included as well.

11

Don't Lose the
Second Generation

By the time Susan had served in her new position for one year, Sonia had recruited Multicultural Partnership Catalysts for three other Parkerite districts. Their monthly online conversations expanded to include the entire team. Susan found it greatly beneficial to interact regularly with others wrestling with the same issues. Each member uniquely contributed to the group.

Sonia facilitated this month's meeting from her hotel room in Nairobi. To accommodate all four time zones in the continental U.S., she had to start the meeting at 9:00 PM her time, after a busy day of meetings in the local office.

Sonia opened the call by summarizing their previous conversations. "We've all grown by interacting with ministry leaders from other cultures. There are now healthy partnerships in several of our districts, serving as role models for all our churches. We've built trusting relationships with believers from Latino, Asian, African, Middle Eastern, and Slavic backgrounds. These create a strong foundation moving forward.

There is a common issue all these ethnic pastors are facing: the loss of their second generations. There are two primary reasons for this. The first has to do with language. For obvious reasons, we first-generation immigrants need to worship in our mother tongues. But our children who grow up in the United States frequently don't. Their heart language is English. Second-generation children of many ethnicities also object that the preaching is too long and focuses on situations they don't experience in America.

The second reason has to do with empowerment for leadership. Western cultures empower women, singles, and young adults for leadership. While America still has a long way to go to reach full equality, it's leaps ahead of the abuse women face daily in India. Most global churches reserve power for older married men. That paradigm is more likely to succeed in their homelands, where it has been the pattern for generations. But in America, their children are taught from first grade to speak up and express themselves. Young single women are making great strides in the classroom and the marketplace—but less so in their parents' churches.

One source of great shame for older immigrant men is the loss of the respect and authority they experienced in their homelands. Many hope they will be able to maintain the culture of deference to the older generations. But few young adults will remain in churches where they are not granted voices in leadership. Some of them choose to attend American churches or launch new multicultural churches. But most simply drop out of church altogether.

So far, we've focused on understanding the cultures of our first-generation partners. That's indispensable, and we must keep at it. But we must also understand the deep chasm between generations within each culture, and what we must do to disciple the second generation in English and empower them as young adults for leadership.

To address this issue, Parker Seminary will be hosting the All Generations Summit next spring. We've already determined some of the keynote speakers, but much of the agenda is still being developed. I hope you will all be able to join us for the summit."

"I hear that Dr. Peter Nnadi will be retiring from Parker next year," said Susan.

"That's right," said Sonia. As the only faculty member of color on the Parker faculty, he will be greatly missed. He won't be completely stepping aside from Parker, but focusing his remaining years on research and writing. But we have good news. Dr. Xie Dong, a native of mainland China, will be joining the Parker faculty this fall. Both Drs. Xie and Nnadi will be speaking at the Summit.

Those are the academic presenters. But we want to highlight pastoral practitioners as well. I'm excited that Pastor Jose Ramirez will be speaking at the summit. Pastor Jose was born in California to a pastoral couple from Uruguay and Venezuela. He pastors Kindred Spirit Church in San Diego. Their services are one hundred percent English, but it's not a typical Anglo church. Kindred Spirit's website describes their services as "English celebration with salsa!" Its very name emphasizes the community all believers can share through our common belonging to the Body of Christ. They've attracted many second- and third-generation Latinos who love their cultural heritage but don't speak Spanish. And because the services are neither stereotypically white nor Latino, they've attracted a wide variety of ethnicities.

Kindred Spirit Church itself has seen strong numerical growth. Even more notably, it has facilitated the launch of a network of second-gen churches that follow its highly relational model. This has resonated more deeply with many second-gen than more programmatically-focused ministries. Who would have ever guessed that the Parkerite Church's most influential ministry model would be spearheaded by a second-generation Latino?

I want to share something with you I need you to keep confidential for a while. Everyone knows that Jose is an up-and-coming leader in the Parkerite Church. While he's a busy pastor, he's assembled a strong team to serve alongside him. That frees up some of his time. We're approaching him about dedicating a percentage of his time to come on denominational staff for the multiplication of second-plus-generation churches among all ethnicities across our districts.

That's a tall order, but Jose is passionate about it. He's connected to second-generation leaders of various ethnicities across the country. They have so much in common, not the least of which is a lack of good role models. Jose is drafting a paradigm of church multiplication among all generations as well as ethnicities across the Parkerite Church.

There are ongoing discussions about the possibility of him taking a part-time role with the denomination. But I've asked him to introduce himself to you by email, as his schedule allows."

That was some of the best news Susan had heard in a long time. She knew of Kindred Spirit Church by reputation, but to hear Jose's story and to think of learning from him was exciting. This news ended their conversation on a high note.

The following morning, Susan was delighted to receive an email from Pastor Jose.

"Dear Susan, it's my honor to introduce myself to you. I'm Jose Ramirez, Pastor of Kindred Spirit Church in the Southern California district of the Parkerite Church. I want to thank you for your sacrificial ministry as Multicultural Partnership Catalyst for the Great Lakes district. Sonia has said such wonderful things about you. I hope it won't be long before we can meet in person. I have a lot to learn from you."

Susan was touched to receive a personal email from such a busy pastor. Clearly this was the kind of person she wanted to learn from. Jose's email continued:

"I've given a lot of thought to how we can multiply healthy Parkerite churches among all generations as well as ethnicities. As you know, it's a complex question. I'm attaching an early draft of a chart that helps me visualize what effective disciple-making among all generations looks like. I'd like to ask for your feedback."

This is going to be interesting, Susan thought. She double-clicked the image to open it.

THE END of Volume 1: ***The Cross-Cultural Partnership Survival Guide.***
If this book sells 1,000 copies, Susan Jamison will return in Volume 2 of the *Connecting Churches Across Cultures series*: ***Christ for All Generations.***

The 7 Day Cross-Cultural Challenge

Looking to cultivate believers passionate about local cross-cultural ministry?
Take **The 7 Day Cross-Cultural Challenge**

The 7 Day Cross-Cultural Challenge is a free series guiding everyday Christians in the initial process of understanding and loving the nations that have moved to their neighborhoods. Each day shares engaging multiple-choice questions, personal challenges, and practical resources. These provide believers with *a **higher** level of* **confidence** in their ability to befriend people of other cultures, engaging their local church in the process.

Try it for yourself. If you're pleased with the results, share **The 7 Day Cross-Cultural Challenge** with your teammates, cultivating their skills in welcoming people of other cultures.

You can register for **The 7 Day Cross-Cultural Challenge** at www.immigrantministry.com/7daychallenge.

The Merging Streams Coalition

Develop your leadership skills beyond mere book learning
Join *The Merging Streams Coalition*

Multiplying healthy partnerships between churches of different cultures

Membership in The Merging Streams Coalition provides individual and small group coaching, alongside monthly live practitioner interviews, video-based lessons, and group prayer gatherings. These resources are delivered at a digestible pace of 3-5 hours per month. The Merging Streams Coalition is not only a place to receive training and coaching, but also to share stories, ideas, resources, networks, and prayer with ministry leaders of diverse denominations, ethnicities, and regions. Many members come not only for their personal development, but also for the identification of resources to develop other leaders in their churches or networks.

The conversations and videos are a huge help for avoiding unnecessary obstacles in ministry, and providing new avenues of thought and mission collaboration. I will use this in my role with our association/district and will recommend others to participate in the Merging Streams Coalition!

Dr. Peter Meier, Executive Director for Missions and Outreach, Lutheran Church Missouri Synod, Florida/Georgia District

You can explore *The Merging Streams Coalition* at
www.immigrantministry.com/mergingstreams.

Implementation Study Guide

Directions: This Implementation Study Guide is not designed as a single-session small group Bible study tool. It is designed to walk local church leadership teams through the process of implementing the principles described in Chapters 6-8. It is recommended that a designated team discuss these questions over time as steps for implementation are determined.

Part 1: Saturating Your Process with United Prayer

The ultimate barrier hindering relationships between believers from different nations isn't cultural, but spiritual. United prayer is necessary to see breakthroughs for healthy cross-cultural church partnerships.

Matthew 18:19-20 "Again I say to you, if two of you agree on earth about anything they ask, it will be done for them by my Father in heaven. For where two or three are gathered in my name, there am I among them."

- Who in your church is united in prayer for the cultivation of healthy cross-cultural church partnerships?
- How will you keep them updated with ongoing prayer requests about specific details of your developing partnership?
- People from different cultures pray very differently, yet their prayers are all welcomed before the throne of God. What Christians from existing or potential partnering churches can pray together in unison for the cultivation of healthy cross-cultural church partnerships?

Part 2: Laying Biblical Foundations

Discuss what obedience to these biblical passages might look like in your church.

Leviticus 19:33-34 "When a stranger sojourns with you in your land, you shall not do him wrong. You shall treat the stranger who sojourns with you as the native among you, and you shall love him as yourself, for you were strangers in the land of Egypt: I am the LORD your God."

When Jesus said the second greatest commandment in the Old Testament was to love your neighbor as yourself, He was specifically quoting a passage from Moses addressing how His people should treat foreigners.

- What grade might God give Old Testament Israelites regarding their obedience to this command?
- What grade might God give the American church regarding our obedience to this command?
- What does it look like to love our neighbors as ourselves in today's society?

Acts 1:8 "You will receive power when the Holy Spirit has come upon you, and you will be my witnesses in Jerusalem, and in all Judea and Samaria, and to the end of the earth."

Judea's majority people were Jewish; they were "people like us." Samaria's majority people were Samaritans; they were "people not like us."

- When you visit your local Walmart, park, or high school, who are the Samaritans you notice?
- If you are aware of churches worshipping in the native languages of your neighbors, what might you do to strengthen those churches?
- If you are not aware of churches worshipping in the native languages of your neighbors, what might you (alone or in cooperation with other area churches) do to reach out to them?

James 1:19 "Let every person be quick to hear, slow to speak, slow to anger."

Americans have a reputation for being talkative, opinionated, and direct. It's easier to develop good listening skills if you know how to ask good questions to draw others out. Schedule unhurried meals for members of your leadership team to ask the following questions of prospective immigrant partners:

- What was it like growing up in your homeland?
- How did you come to the United States?
- How are your children doing?
- How did you plant your church?
- What's difficult about pastoring in the U.S.?
- How might American Christians walk alongside you in ministry?

After you've had a few of these conversations, return as a group and discuss these questions:

- What did you learn through these conversations?
- What does your church need to change to better serve your immigrant neighbors?
- What opportunities for shared ministry did you discover?
- How can you continue to be good listeners in your ongoing relationships with these believers?

Cast a Compelling Vision

- How might you adapt the message of Chapter 6 to fit your unique voice?
- Chapter 6 told the stories of role model churches in the Minneapolis area. What stories of healthy cross-cultural churches can you identify from your city or denomination?
- Who is passionate about this vision, and able to be part of the team promoting it?
- What means will you use to promote the vision (platform, social media, bulletin, website, small groups, etc.)?

Building a Small but Healthy Team

Below are necessary qualities of the Three Indispensable Persons. Which of these are already present, and which are lacking? How might this be addressed?

- The senior American pastor
- Fully embraces the vision
- Serves as the primary vision caster

- Needs good personal chemistry with the immigrant church's senior immigrant pastor
- Is learning the differences between expressions of worship and obedience between his and his partner church's cultures
- Theologically and morally conservative (because your immigrant partner most likely will be)
- The American church's Connector
- Highly values the opportunity to befriend someone of another culture
- Agrees to meet monthly or more often with the lead immigrant pastor
- Is developing good listening and question-asking skills
- Needs good personal chemistry with the senior pastors of both churches
- The senior immigrant pastor
- Theologically orthodox
- Desires to partner with believers of other ethnicities
- Open to discipling his church's children in English and empowering them as young adults for leadership
- Needs good personal chemistry with the American church's senior pastor and Connector
- Agrees to meet monthly or more often with the American church's Connector

Which of these steps for vetting potential partnering churches have you completed?

- Leaders from both churches attend each other's services
- Both senior pastors and the Connector share a meal together

- Discuss alignment regarding theology, mission, and vision
- United prayer

Have you had one-on-one conversations with members of your Board, staff, and congregation who may be early adopters of this vision? Have you had one-on-one conversations with those who may be resistant?

Conducting a Simple, Small-Scale Launch Event

Who are the people from the leadership teams of both churches who will work together at every step of the development of this launch event? When is the best time of the week for them to meet? What means of communication will be necessary for all of them to be included (email, text, social media, etc.)?

- What are your team's decisions about *choosing* the event?
- What are your team's decisions about *planning* the event? What are the different elements of the event, and who needs to be involved in planning each one?
- What are your team's decisions about *funding* the event? How will you determine appropriate amounts for each church to contribute?
- What are your team's decisions about *conducting* the event? How will you ensure that as many people from both churches as possible engage in each aspect of the event?
- What are your team's decisions about *celebrating* the event? Can the celebration be held at the conclusion of the event, or is a later gathering more appropriate?

- What are your team's decisions about *evaluating* the event? What does each church see as success? As less than success?
- What are your team's decisions about *expanding* the event? If the evaluation of your event was positive overall, members of both churches should discuss options for establishing regularly reoccurring events or establishing ongoing ministry programming.

What steps has the American church taken to engage these groups of people?

- Active members
- Lapsed members
- Youth and young adults

Does your partnership require a Church Facility Stewardship Covenant? If so, have you adopted the Covenant in this book to fit your context?

Would it be wise for you to hold an inauguration service to publicly acknowledge and pray over the formation of your partnership? If so, what elements would make that service meaningful to both churches?

Template for a Church Facility Stewardship Covenant

There are several similarities between two people entering a marriage and two churches entering an agreement regarding the shared use of space. There will be fewer surprises if both parties get to know one another and draw healthy boundaries before entering the relationship. Below are pertinent questions regarding a church facility stewardship covenant between two churches.

Who owns the facility?

In one sense, this question asks whether the facility is owned by the local congregation, the denomination, or the bank (if there is a mortgage). Hopefully all will agree, however, that the facility is ultimately *property of Jesus Christ*. If Jesus is the ultimate owner of the facility and those using it are all stewards, then both host and guest congregations will strive to steward the facility well for the expansion of His Kingdom.

Who will manage the ongoing relationship?

Any facility usage covenant is only as good as the relationship between the two responsible persons who maintain ongoing communication. Connectors from each church should spend at least five hours per month in dialogue, discussing personal as well as business matters. In addition to two Connectors, churches sharing facilities should designate an English-speaking person from each church as the responsible party. The responsible party for each church may be the same persons as the Connectors, or not. The two responsible persons should share cell phone numbers for the resolution of ongoing issues as they arise.

How will you manage cultural differences in facility usage?

Two parties acting in good faith to steward a facility will naturally follow their own cultural guidelines for doing so. These guidelines are typically unwritten and assumed. Americans may assume that children should not be left unattended at any time, while global cultures may view unattended children as perfectly natural. Some American churches require criminal background checks to protect children from sexual predators. Many global cultures may feel that this smacks of distrust and will be especially concerning for those whose citizenship papers are in process.

How will both churches be publicly recognized?

If La Casa del Padre begins to meet at the facility of Redeemer Lutheran Church, both sides should agree how each should be listed on the church website and other public media. If La Casa del Padre is not governed by the Board of Redeemer Lutheran, it should not be listed as Redeemer's

1:00 pm service, Spanish-language service, or Latino outreach. It should be listed publicly as La Casa del Padre unless its leadership indicates otherwise.

How should we develop our Church Facility Stewardship Covenant?

This document does not need to be a legal contract. Conversations regarding the Covenant should involve the leadership of both congregations. An exception can be made if the host church sees itself as simply a landlord. In that case, the host church can unilaterally write a Covenant and present it to a potential tenant. The covenant may need to be bilingual. If this is a ministry partnership, the document should be signed by both lead pastors during the services of both congregations. This can be accompanied by joint celebration and prayer over the newly-formed partnership.

Below is a template for a Church Facility Steward Covenant that can be adapted for your context.

Template for a Church Facility Stewardship Covenant

Church Facility Stewardship Covenant between _____ (host church name) and _____ (guest church name).

Based on our mutual love for Christ and one another, we agree to serve together for the advancement of the Kingdom of God. As brothers and sisters in Christ, we commit to keep the terms of this covenant to the best of our abilities. We both want to be good stewards of this church facility, believing its ultimate owner is our Lord Jesus Christ. We will hold each other in high regard, working through tensions in kindness, not providing bitterness with any opportunity to fester between us.

We agree to hold monthly conversations between _____ (host church's Connector) and _____ (guest church's Connector).

(Omit this line if the usage of the facility is rent-free) The guest church agrees that a sum of $____ per (month/year/etc.) be paid the host church for the use of its facility.

- Here are our agreements regarding which areas of the host church will be accessible to the guest church, including the use of the parking lot _____

- Here are our agreements regarding the fixed times the guest church may use the host church facility, and the method and advance notification needed to request one-time events, including who must be notified _____

- Here are our agreements regarding keys or access cards, who can make copies of them and give them to whom _____

- Here are our agreements regarding children being supervised or unsupervised, areas open to children, and required criminal background checks for those who serve children _____

- Here are our agreements regarding use of the sound system, computers, and other technologies _____

- Here are our agreements regarding heating and air conditioning _____

- Here are our agreements regarding cleaning after each use of the facility, disposal of trash, and liability for spills, stains, and damage to facilities, including the responsible parties

_____

- Here are our agreements regarding the use of kitchen, refrigerator, and dining areas, including what a church kitchen should smell like

_____

- Here are our agreements regarding liability insurance _____
- Here are our agreements regarding how the host church will represent the guest church on its website and other public media _____
- Here are our agreements concerning the communication of this agreement to the members of both congregations _____

Signatures

Host church pastor name _____
Signature _____
Date _____

Guest church pastor name _____
Signature _____
Date _____

Host church Connector name _____
Signature _____
Date _____

Guest church Connector name _____
Signature _____
Date _____

Translator name (if necessary) _____
Signature _____
Date _____

Recommended Digital and Print Resources

Digital Resources

Because many global cultures prefer oral learning, it's important to identify video-based disciple-making resources in multiple languages. Immigrant Ministry Connections lists directories of organizations providing multilingual disciple-making media at www.immigrantministry.com/resources, as well as other online resources including:

- Bibles in over 4,000 languages
- Best websites for beginners
- Directories of hundreds of local ministry nonprofit agencies serving in all 50 states and all 13 provinces and territories of Canada
- Directories of ministries training in specific skills such as making disciples, teaching English, refugee resettlement, international student ministry, and more

Print Resources

A Future for the Latino Church by Daniel A. Rodriguez and Manuel Ortiz (InterVarsity Press, 2011)

An exploration of reasons why English-language worship is essential to discipling second-plus-generation Latinos, with observations regarding several ministry models

Against All Odds: The Struggle for Racial Integration in Religious Organizations by Brad Christerson, Korie L. Edwards, and Michael O. Emerson (New York University Press, 2004)

Case studies of churches, nonprofits, and one college demonstrating the difficulty of maintaining long-term cohesion within multicultural ministries

Ethnic Blends by Mark DeYmaz and Harry Li (Zondervan, 2010)

An excellent introduction to the planting and development of multicultural congregations

Growing Healthy Asian American Churches by Peter Cha, S. Steve Kang, and Helen Lee (InterVarsity Press, 2006)

A project written by a group of Asian American ministry leaders discussing the planting and maintenance of healthy Asian American churches

Hope for the Second Generation by Tesfai Tesema (Tenthpower Publishing, 2022)

A first-generation Ethiopian pastor explores reasons the second generation is leaving the church, and proposes the planting of networks of English-language second-generation Ethiopian-led multicultural churches

The New Pilgrims by Joseph Castleberry (Worthy Books, 2015)

Stories of Christian Latino immigrants to the United States whose contribution to American spiritual development leads the author to compare them to the Pilgrim fathers

One Body, One Spirit by George Yancey (InterVarsity Press, 2003)

Principles for building multicultural congregations based on nationwide research conducted by The Lilly Endowment

Our Children Need Roots and Wings by Harvey C. Kwyani (Missio Africanus, 2019)

An immigrant to Britain from Malawi explores why most immigrant churches close at the end of one generation, as well as kinds of ministries necessary to attract the second generation

Pursuing the Pearl by Ken Uyeda Fong (Judson Press, 1999)

A third-generation Chinese-American explores the need and process for planting churches specifically designed for third-plus-generation Asian Americans

Silent Exodus by Steve Pinto (Xulon Press, 2021)

A first-generation Colombian immigrant shares the story and statistical results of his church's launch of an all-English service serving second-plus generation Latinos

Under One Steeple by Lorraine Cleaves Anderson (Wipf & Stock, 2012)

An overview of the multi-congregational church, defined as multiple congregations sharing more than just space

Understanding the Coconut Generation by Sam George (Mall Publishing, 2006)

A first-generation immigrant from India explores reasons the second generation typically leave their parents' churches, and models of ministry that will appeal to them.

About the Author

John Wesley Yoder is Founder and Director of Immigrant Ministry Connections, coaching denominational leaders and pastors in cultivating healthy cross-cultural church partnerships.

John has worshipped in over 80 diverse immigrant churches across the Minneapolis area, meeting their pastors and listening to their stories. At the same time, he has dialogued with ministry leaders nationwide about the blessings and challenges of partnerships between American and immigrant churches.

Over time, these conversations led to the creation of blogs, networking directories, online courses, and other resources at www.immigrantministry.com.

John has pastored in a large multicultural church in Beijing, China, and trained pastors across Asia. He is a graduate of Liberty Baptist Theological Seminary, an ordained minister of The Evangelical Free Church of America and has been happily married to Sherry for 27 years.

The author should not be confused with John Howard Yoder, author of *The Politics of Jesus* and other books, who passed away in 1997.

Questions may be directed to the author at:
john@immigrantministry.com.

Notes

6. Quick Start Guideline 1: Cast a Compelling Vision

1. https://cis.org/Report/Birth-Rates-Among-Immigrants-America
2. https://research.lifeway.com/wp-content/uploads/2023/01/Hispanic-American-Church-Study-Report.pdf
3. https://lausanne.org/occasional-paper/lop-1
4. https://ag.org/About/Statistics